𝕿𝖍𝖊 𝕯𝖆𝖎𝖑𝖞

THE
LAKE DISTRICT
in a week

NIGEL RICHARDSON

*Head*way · Hodder & Stoughton

Acknowledgements

The author and publishers are grateful to: J Allan Cash Ltd for the photograph
on the Front cover; Cars of the Stars Motor Museum for the photograph on
p 29; Mike Williams for the photograph on p 92 and David Mossman for all
other photographs used in this book except those on pp 4, 24, 26, 41, 101 which
were taken by the author.

Maps created by Alan Gilliland and Glenn Swann

The *Journals of Dorothy Wordsworth* are available in Oxford Paperbacks
*Home at Grasmere: Extracts from the Journals of Dorothy Wordsworth and from the
Poems of William Wordsworth* is available in Penguin Classics
Recollections of the Lakes and the Lake Poets by Thomas De Quincey is available in
Penguin Classics

Front cover: Loweswater
Back cover: River Derwent, Borrowdale

British Library Cataloguing in Publication Data
Richardson, Nigel
"Daily Telegraph" The Lake District in a Week
("Daily Telegraph" Travel in a Week Series)
I. Title II. Series
914.27804

ISBN 0 340 58312 6

First published 1993
Third impression 1993

© 1993 The Telegraph plc

Printed in Italy for the educational publishing division of Hodder & Stoughton
Ltd, Mill Road, Dunton Green, Sevenoaks, Kent by New Interlitho, Milan.

THE LAKE DISTRICT IN A WEEK

Introduction

This guide is designed for visitors touring the Lake District by car who wish to see the best the region has to offer in the limited time at their disposal. We have divided the Lakes into seven areas, each of which can easily be covered in a day's drive. Within each of these 'Days' the most interesting places to visit, from the lakes themselves to the incomparable fells and Lakeland towns and villages, have been listed as a menu of options, arranged in alphabetical order for easy reference. From the Day's menu you can choose the attractions which hold most appeal, depending on the weather, your interests, and whether you are travelling with children. Symbols placed alongside the text will aid you in your choice.

The Lake District is the most popular tourist centre in Britain and there are hundreds of attractions and things to do. The aim of this guide is to give a critical appraisal of the most popular and help you discover some of the region's hidden gems. Our assessments will give you a clear idea of what you can expect to see, the best time of day and year to visit and, where admission is charged, whether the attractions offer value for money. As well as covering the main towns and tourist honeypots, we have highlighted small gems in each area, from lonely and atmospheric valleys to unusual shops and good places for lunch.

A walk of the day in each area is described in detail. Most are just over one hour long and provide an opportunity to get out of the car and stretch your legs. We have also included descriptions of particularly interesting and scenic drives. At the end of each Day we have given suggestions for places to stay, from country house hotels to guesthouses, and places to eat, from the best restaurants to pubs with good home-made fare.

CONTENTS

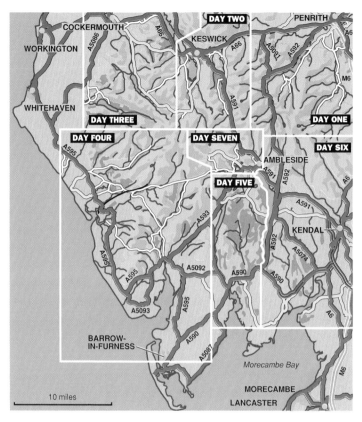

KEY TO SYMBOLS

- ⊕ Star Attraction
- ☆ Well worth a visit
- ☆ Of interest
- 🚶 Walk of the day
- ---- Route of walk
- 🚗 Drive of the day
- ═══ Route of drive
- ☀ Fine weather attraction
- 🌧 Wet weather attraction
- 🚶 Enjoyable for children
- ⓘ Tourist Information Centre
- ◉ Lunch/snack stop
- 🏠 Hotel
- 🏠 Guesthouse
- SC Self-catering accommodation
- ✕ Restaurant
- 🍺 Pub with good food
- 🍺 Pub with accommodation

- 🚶5 Children allowed (number = from which age)
- 🐕 Dogs allowed
- ▭ Credit cards accepted
- ▧ Credit cards not accepted
- **£** Bed and breakfast under £17 per person; three-course meal under £10 a head
- **££** Bed and breakfast £18-£35 per person; three-course meal £11-£16 a head
- **£££** Bed and breakfast £36-£49 per person; three-course meal £17-£24 a head
- **££££** Bed and breakfast over £50 per person; three-course meal over £25 a head

v

Sunrise over Grasmere

Lodore Falls

Esthwaite Water

Sheep at Cockley Beck

ULLSWATER

Wordsworth's daffodils grew on the shore here; now the idea of wandering lonely as a cloud is strictly a pipedream during the summer months. Ullswater's proximity to the M6 and the Yorkshire Dales makes it a honeypot for tourists, but not even the high summer traffic gridlock on the shoreline road can quite detract from the sinuous beauty of the lake. And people tend to forget that in Penrith Ullswater has on its doorstep one of the finest, least spoilt little towns in the north-west.

The round-the-lake boat trips aboard restored Victorian steamers will give you the full picture of Ullswater from its mountains in the south-west to the gently sloping hills towards Penrith. There are some classic low-level leisurely strolls to Aira Force waterfall and along the shore from Howtown to Glenridding, as well as more serious fellwalks on Martindale Common and around the head of Haweswater reservoir. But if the weather closes in, or the children prefer more spoonfed forms of enjoyment, there is a wealth of attractions close at hand.

Lowther Leisure Park combines a tranquil parkland setting with all the fun of the fair. Dalemain House will keep you dry amid a warren of rooms tunnelling back through the Georgian period to the mediaeval days of border skirmishes between the Scots and the English. And if it is peace and seclusion you're really after, you'll find it on even the busiest day by seeking out the remote Swindale Valley beyond Haweswater. The tourists never quite reach this far, so don't tell anyone about it.

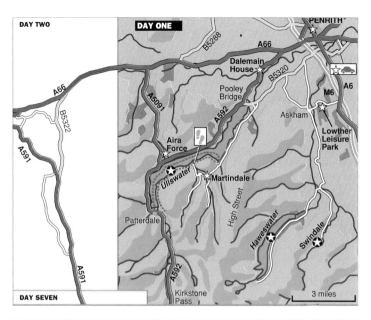

☆ **AIRA FORCE**

The Lake District's many waterfalls pulse with the timeless power of the fells and there couldn't be a more appropriate name for them than the Old Norse word 'force'. There are higher and wilder falls than Aira Force, which is wedged into a wooded gorge on the north shore of Ullswater, but none has Aira's parkland setting and picturesque viewing points.

From the main car park the path leads through the valley of Aira Beck, planted with pines and firs, including monkey puzzles, and the perfect climate (sheltered and damp) for rare mosses, lichens and ferns. Go over the beck (look out for the tree-branch by the wooden bridge which has grown in an extraordinary parabola in its quest for light) and double back along the side of the valley ignoring the rising path to the right. Presently you will reach the first of two lovely old flint bridges at the foot and head of Aira Force itself. This lower bridge faces the 65-foot falls full on while the upper arch has vertiginous views of the water pumping down through its funnel of smooth glistening rocks. From the top bridge follow the western edge of the boulder-strewn beck as far as High Force, which is wide and shallow

where Aira is narrow and tall. The wooden gate by these falls
will take you across a field (good views of High Dodd and Place
Fell on the south shore of Ullswater) and back to the waterfall
area.

Aira Force

Follow the signs from the car park for the **Aira Force Tea Rooms** which offer light lunches (toasted sandwiches, soup and roll), excellent carrot cake and Westmoreland tea bread, and tables with views down to Ullswater shore - at least when the trees aren't too leafy.

The National Trust car park for Aira Force is on the A592 (Ullswater shore road) 2¹⁄₂ miles from Glenridding near the junction with the A5091. There's a charge for parking which includes a free explanatory leaflet. If this car park is full there's another up the hill on the A5091

Opening times: Aira Force itself is always accessible. The tea rooms are open daily 9.30am-6.30pm in season or when the weather is fine; otherwise weekends only

☆ DALEMAIN HOUSE

Modern realities have forced many aristocrats to open parts of their country piles to nosy *hoi polloi* like us; Dalemain is no exception. For three centuries it has been the home of the Hassell family and everywhere there are portraits of family members, most of them called Edward, to remind you of the fact.

The rather boring façade added in 1750 hides an Elizabethan manor house and, behind that, a Norman pele-tower containing a labyrinth of passages and rooms. The fretwork plaster ceiling on the panelled first floor is Tudor and it's worth risking neck-crick to admire the embossed roses, fleur-de-lys and bunches of acorns. The priest's hiding hole at the back of the housekeeper's room was built after the Reformation by previous owners who were staunch Roman Catholics and access used to be via the kitchen chimney - the kitchen fire would be lit below once a fugitive had escaped there, which gives new meaning to the phrase 'saved by the seat of your pants'. Children should look out for Mrs Mouse's House on the way out - but we're not saying where.

Out in the courtyard the magnificent 16th-century loft-barn houses a collection of agricultural and household bygones - those that haven't made it onto the walls of the Lake District's inns and pubs - and in another outhouse there's a rather disappointing museum of rural tools and stuffed birds. The gardens hold far more interest and include a Tudor gazebo with pointed timber roof, terraced walks, a knot garden originally laid out on the same pattern as the fretwork ceiling in the pele-tower, and a wild area of gnarled old trees and flowering shrubs.

The **tearoom** in the mediaeval Old Hall is worth a visit for the privilege of drinking in its atmosphere of simple antiquity along with your tea. There are also lunchtime specials such as lamb chops, delicious home-made cakes, and, to take away, gooseberry and elderflower jam and applemint jelly.

Dalemain House is on the A592 midway between the north end of Ullswater and Penrith
Opening times: Easter Sun-first Sun in Oct, Sun-Thurs 11.15am-5pm
Admission: for house, museums and gardens - adult £3.50; child £2.50; family ticket £9.50; gardens and museums only - adult £2.50; child free

Small Water tarn with Haweswater in background

✪ HAWESWATER

 Haweswater is a reservoir, and something of a plain Jane compared to the raving beauties of Derwentwater or Ullswater. But it still gets over-run, thanks to the twin attractions of the drowned village of Mardale - periodically visible when the water level drops - and the only nesting pair of Golden Eagles in England.

Access for the droves of rubberneckers hoping for a glimpse of these phenomena is confined to a single-track, dead-end road. According to one local, 'if you started a small business you could make a fortune putting bumpers and wing mirrors back on'.

Still, the walking - and the prospect of a glimpse of those magnificent eagles - are powerful magnets. From the car park at the head of the lake there are long-distance walks up on to the ridge-top Roman route known as High Street. To reach it take the right-hand path signposted for the village of Bampton via the north-west shore of the lake, then follow signs off to the left. The path straight ahead goes to Kentmere via a tarn called Small Water (there are excellent views of the head of the lake and the beck coiling into it), and the left-hand path takes you to Longsleddale via the Gatescarth Pass.

During the nesting season (spring and early summer) the RSPB maintains an observation post manned by wardens to keep an eye on the Golden Eagles. Anyone stumbling across the post will be welcomed by the wardens and may be lucky enough to actually observe the splendid golden eagles, but for obvious reasons the RSPB would prefer not to disclose the exact whereabouts of the post.

After the rigours and remoteness of Haweswater, the best place to recharge your batteries is at the **Punchbowl Inn** in the picturesque stone-built village of Askham on the way back to Penrith. It is as welcoming inside as its rangy 18th-century exterior suggests. There's a spacious main lounge with open log fire and a more formal restaurant at the back with fascinating old photographs of the Haweswater dam under construction and Mardale before the valley was flooded to make the reservoir. Apart from the usual pub fare there's French smokehouse quail, Swiss Bratwurst, vegetarian pasta or, for those brave and carnivorous enough, Nick's Platter: steak, Cumberland sausage, lamb chop, pork cutlet, bacon, lamb's liver, tomatoes, mushrooms and egg. There's also a 'Kids' Korner' menu offering mini pizzas, bacon nuggets and the like. Food is served in the winter noon-2pm and 7-9pm (9.30pm in summer); Sundays 7-9.30pm.

☆ LOWTHER LEISURE PARK

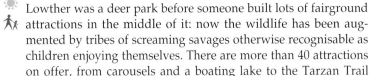

Lowther was a deer park before someone built lots of fairground attractions in the middle of it: now the wildlife has been augmented by tribes of screaming savages otherwise recognisable as children enjoying themselves. There are more than 40 attractions on offer, from carousels and a boating lake to the Tarzan Trail

Assault Course, climbing tubes, the BMX Bike Track and the Aqua Blaster Water Cannon Game (the more dangerous rides are supervised). There's also a Big Top with circus performances twice daily featuring trapeze artistes, clowns and a rubber lady. All rides bar a handful are included in the entry price so it will not burn too much of a hole in your pocket, but adults still have the problem of how to occupy their time if the trampolines don't appeal. The complex of self-service cafeteria, licensed restaurant and bar is pretty shoddy and should be avoided - far better to pack a picnic and head out on foot into the deer park where you should find a secluded spot in the shade of a tree. Then all you need is a pair of earplugs to screen out the warcries of childish delight.

Lowther Leisure Park, Hackthorpe (just off the A6 five miles south of Penrith).
Tel: 09312 523
Opening times: vary, but usually 2 wks either side of Easter; weekends only in May except Bank Hols; daily June 1-Sept 12 10am-5pm, an hour later on fine summer days; last admission an hour before closing time
Admission: adult and child over 3 £4.95

MARTINDALE

Here is one of those places to be quiet awhile and absorb the true splendour of the fells and valleys. Martindale Old Church is the place to head for, a left turn past the New Church on the dead-end road to the head of the valley. The Old Church has stood here since the time of the Armada. Nothing much has changed down the centuries. The single row of pews on either side face inwards across the stone-flagged floor. The sole source of light is a candle on the lectern.

Outside there's a wisp of smoke from the solitary farmhouse beyond the stone bridge over the beck, the barking of a border collie and the massive cleavage of the valley head; only the tractor by the farmhouse fixes the scene in the 20th century...if you're lucky enough to be alone, that is. Unfortunately unless you get there early in the morning or at dusk (a particularly atmospheric time) you might well find yourself in the company of scores of other car-bound mystics, for this is an incredibly popular route with motorists and there's no such thing as a well kept secret in the Lake District.

A haven of peace: Martindale Old Church

☆ PENRITH

This former capital of the ancient State of Cumbria covets its position just beyond the boundary of the Lake District National Park and doesn't want its considerable charms advertised too loudly. Few shops obviously cater for tourists, and though the town is well stocked with guesthouses Penrith has retained its air of a thriving market town. One way to appreciate the town centre is to follow a leaflet, 'Penrith Town Trail', available for 20p from the **Tourist Information Centre** in Middlegate (tel: 0768 67466), though strangely it misses out most of the highlights listed below. The Tourist Information Centre is an extension of the former Robinson's School, built in Elizabethan times and now housing the rather disappointing **Penrith Museum.** If 'sugar nippers given by JMR Dodd', a 'pair of wooden pattens' looking more like last summer's espadrilles and other odds and ends trawled from local attics are your kind of thing, linger awhile.

Otherwise head south-east down **Middlegate** towards the centre, and notice as you go the 'yards' feeding into it, a feature of many Border towns in England and Scotland which suffered centuries of unexpected attacks. When the alarm was raised, the inhabitants would drive their livestock and families through these yards and into the safety of the town thoroughfares. The lintel above Williamson Yard next to Woolworth's bears the inscription 'RLE 1697' and some strange symbols, one of which probably represents sheep shears.

A wonderfully old-fashioned haberdashers called **Arnisons** stands at the head of Devonshire Street (as it has for centuries, judging by the window displays). At about 12 feet wide the road through here was just about the narrowest part of the main road to Scotland before the M6 was opened. Further up in Market Square stands the imposing façade of the grocer's shop, **James and John Graham**, which styles itself 'Agricultural seedcake and manure merchants, Italian warehousemen, tea and provision merchants' and has been trading there since 1793. Inside the timbered room with its stained glass windows the aroma is heady (and thankfully untinged by manure), a blend of coffee from Java, curing hams, game pie and Polish sausage. And standing behind the counter in the middle the butcher wears apron and side whiskers...truly the elegance, style and service of a bygone era.

The **Two Lions Hotel** in Great Dockray, where Penrith's Tuesday street markets are held, offers a happy combination of history and hearty food. The former home of local bigwig Gerard Lowther, a forebear of the Earls of Lonsdale, it dates from the 16th century. There's a functional restaurant at the back, but the best place to eat - if it's not a Tuesday and full of drinkers from the market - is the bar at the front. The magnificent, geometrically designed ceiling (rather like the one in Dalemain House) is horsehair and plaster and dates from 1584. The fireplace bears the date 1585; and the ancient wooden alcoves must be of similar vintage. Rack of lamb, beef Stroganoff and steak and kidney pie are staples - but there's a decent selection of salads and some unusual specials such as prawn and pineapple curry. Children can choose from the 'Lion's Cub Menu' which has pizza, sausage or beefburger, all with chips, for under £2. Food is served daily noon-2pm and 6.30-11pm; Sundays 7-10.30pm.

The old foundry in Castlegate now houses the **Penrith Steam Museum**, which is more interesting than it may sound. Apart from the impressive collection of traction engines, boilers, model steam engines and old motorbikes, there's a working blacksmith and some fascinating reminders of the building's former use as a foundry. The Stalker Brothers who set up the foundry in 1851 diversified from the manufacture of ploughs and threshing machines .into boilers and iron and brass founding as the Industrial Revolution gathered momentum. The pattern shop stores the original wooden moulds and the blacksmith in residence still uses many of the tools from the 1850s. The old foundry office has been left intact, with its leather-bound ledgers and ancient typewriter, and one of the old ironworker's cottages has been refurbished as it was at the turn of the century.

Penrith Steam Museum, Castlegate. Tel: 0768 62154
Opening times: Easter weekend & Spring Bank Hol-end Sept, Mon-Fri 10am-4.30pm
(last admission)
Admission: adult £1.50; child 75p

☆ PENRITH DRIVE

  Just south of Penrith are a number of historical sites best visited in a single drive. Take the A6 from the roundabout at the southern end of the town. Half a mile along turn right up the B5320 to Pooley Bridge, just by an ancient monument known as Arthur's Round Table. A short distance up on the right is a turn signposted **Mayburgh Henge** and Southwaite Green, which is as near the southbound carriageway of the M6 as you get without being on the hard shoulder. There's a lay-by for parking opposite a gate, and a path leads up a bank to the lip of the earthwork. Mayburgh now consists of a single stone (in the 18th century there were at least eight stones) standing in the centre of a natural grassy bowl 120 metres across. In any other place it would be unremarkable, but the juxtaposition of old and new - the mournful abandonment of this lonely megalith contrasting with the incessant noise of the motorway traffic - makes it a poignant sight.

Return to the A6, turn right and take the first left on the B6262. Just beyond a little bridge and chapel is the car park for

Brougham Hall. This former home of the family that gave its name to the Brougham carriage has an eccentric history and no-one is better equipped to tell it than the man who fell in love with the hall when it was a pile of rubble and set about rebuilding it. When he is not in hard hat and overalls doing his bit for the restoration, Christopher Terry is talking enthusiastically about the past. The hall was the site of the last battle on English soil (Bonny Prince Charlie *versus* the English, 1745) and the 19th-century landspeed record (achieved in a Brougham carriage laden with batteries). In 1932 the fourth Lord Brougham twice broke the bank at Monte Carlo and then proceeded to break his family by squandering a fortune of £16 million by the age of 21. Brougham was then sold for demolition and later used during the Second World War to develop a top secret weapon, the Canal Light Defence Tank. Finally, Terry himself rode to the rescue in 1985 when he set up a charitable trust to restore the place and turn it into a complex of workshops for local craftsmen.

The completion of the project is still two or three years off, and meanwhile the hall is an intriguing blend of dereliction and pristine restoration, like 'before' and 'after' pictures spliced together. Workshops already in place include The Old Smokehouse, where fish, meat and game are traditionally oak-smoked, a goldsmith and jeweller, a metalworker and a woodturner, and there are also plans for a children's educational museum on the geology, flora and fauna of the Lake District. Grab a chat with Christopher Terry if you can - he'll be the one working the hardest.

Brougham Hall on the B6262 between the A6 and the A66 south-east of Penrith
Opening times: the Hall itself never closes; The Old Smokehouse (0768 67772) open
Tues-Sun 10am-5.30pm and Bank Hols; Goldsmith and jeweller Mark Heeley-Creed
(0768 66363) open Thurs-Sun, times vary; John Harrison's metalwork studio (0768
890558) open every day, times vary; Woodturner Walter Gundrey (0434 381563) open
Sun-Thurs 11am-6.30pm

Further up the B6262, a left turn towards the A66 brings you to **Brougham Castle.** Situated by the lovely River Eamont - and the not-so-lovely A66 - the castle is one of many pink sandstone fortifications in these parts built to stem the tide of southward-tending Scots. The river crossing here had strategic importance from the time the Romans built a fort (its outlines are visible in the field next to the castle) and Brougham would be hardly worth the visit if it weren't for the collection of Roman milestones and tombstones housed in the English Heritage hut in the castle courtyard.

The castle's other highlight is the keep, whose weathered spiral staircase is the stuff of children's adventure stories. On the top floor it opens onto a walled gallery that leads round three sides of the keep to a secretive private chapel whose trefoiled windows are carved with exquisitely executed Victorian graffiti. The information booklet available in the ticket office is only worth the 75p if you long to know the comparatively unremarkable history of the place.

Brougham Castle is just off the A66 a mile or so south-east of Penrith. Tel: 0768 62488
Opening times: Apr-Sept Tues-Sun 10am-6pm, rest of year Wednes-Sun 10am-4pm
Admission: adult £1.10; child 5-16 55p

Brougham Hall

SWINDALE

This bleak, other-worldly valley on the far side of Haweswater is the perfect place to escape the crowds and clogged roads. It is rarely visited, even in high summer, and seems to retain its own forbidding and windy climate whatever the weather elsewhere.

In fact you are more likely to encounter hunting parties than tourists (the road is narrow and it can be tricky reversing in the face of a convoy of Land Rovers full of baying dogs and men with shotguns). Drive through Bampton and Bampton Grange, then take the right fork: Swindale is signposted three miles by the cattlegrid. Continue past a water pumping station and two more grids, following the course of Swindale Beck. Park just before a farm on the verge near a pumping sub-station (the road continues to another farm but there is nowhere to park). Follow the road on foot, past the second farm that must rank as one of the loneliest spots in Christendom - well, England anyway. From here take the bridleway rather than the Old Corpse Road (which takes you over Swindale Common to the south end of Haweswater). Presently you reach a landscape of lunar bleakness enclosed by the head of the valley where there are two waterfalls - one incising a deep wound in the crag, the other slaloming more gently. Here in this natural bowl there are hummocks of puzzling provenance, a rocky outcrop standing at the entrance like a sentinel, and in the middle a tomb-like stone surrounded by trees. You may find a sheltered spot among the hummocks for a picnic; otherwise, gaze and enjoy.

✪   ULLSWATER

The most beautiful of the lakes, so they say, though each has its special qualities of scenery and atmosphere. Ullswater is nine miles long and certainly the bendiest, almost like an upside-down question-mark. This makes for fascinating, constantly shifting perspectives if you drive east on the A592 along its north shore and pause at the several stopping places. Ullswater's southern end is dominated by fells sloping up into the Hellvellyn range. The most dramatic way to set eyes on Ullswater for the first time is to approach it from the south, along the A592 via Kirkstone Pass. The northern approach, from Penrith, is much flatter and less dramatic. Ullswater's rather tatty villages - Patterdale and Glenridding in the south and Pooley Bridge at the northern tip - do scant justice to the surroundings and are not worth much of your time. Far better to take advantage of the many walks or get out on the lake itself, whether by rowing boat, motor boat, yacht or steamer.

Brothers Water from Kirkstone Pass

Glenridding Sailing School and Boat Hire (07684 82541; access road between the Ullswater and Glenridding Hotels) is open 10am-5pm end Mar-end Oct. There are a variety of vessels for hire.
Tindals Boat Hire, Glenridding (07684 82393), just south of the steamer pier by the snack bar, has 4-seater motorboats for £11 an hour; rowing boats £6 an hour
Ullswater's Victorian steamers Raven and Lady of the Lake, with their jaunty red funnels, ply the length of the lake in season from Glenridding to Pooley Bridge and back, stopping at Howtown, a return trip of two hours. The full service runs 2 wks either side of Easter, May Bank Hol, and mid-May - end Sept. Sailings depart 10am-4.30pm from Glenridding (last sailing from Pooley Bridge 5.30pm). Out of season and in poor weather it is advisable to check times with the Ullswater Navigation and Transit Co (0539 721626 or 07684 82229). Round the Lake tickets: adult £4.50; child £2.50; family ticket for 5 £11.30

LAKESHORE WALK

The steamer-ride from Glenridding to Howtown and shoreline walk back has a deserved reputation for being one of the finest days out in the Lake District. It is best to resign yourself to doing it with hordes of others and enjoy the camaraderie. Many people take picnics - there are some excellent picnicking spots along the way - but you should take something to drink at the very least as the return walk from Howtown is a good six miles.

Board the steamer at Glenridding pier. She'll drop you in Howtown in 40 minutes by which time you'll have seen the best of the lake (the full round trip to Pooley Bridge can drag a bit). The steamers are elegant on the outside, functional inside. You can sit under the canopy or lounge on the sun deck.

Disembark at Howtown's small wooden pier. The Howtown Hotel straight ahead up the road will do take-away sandwiches if you've forgotten to pack any. Otherwise turn right off the boat (with all the other people) and follow the shore path which presently climbs a hill to a wooden gate where you turn right on to the main footpath. By turning left here you can make a detour to the top of Hallin Fell (1,271ft), a vigorous 40-minute walk there and back but well worth the panoramic views that on a clear day might extend to the Pennines, 25 miles to the east.

The views are stunning enough, though, on the basic low level walk. Looking back before you round the headland there are uninterrupted views of the north-east finger of the lake right down to Pooley Bridge. Eventually you reach a hillside ringed by miniature fells. Take care not to trip over the picnickers who congregate here (there are excellent views of the lake if you climb the hillside high enough). The path continues past a waterfall and follows the contours of the lakeshore. When you reach the A592, turn right to return to the car park at Glenridding pier - or left to a recommended hostelry.

The **White Lion Inn** at Patterdale has the singular virtue of serving food all day, every day, from noon to 10pm except Sundays when it is closed 3-7pm. No children are allowed inside after 8pm. From the outside it looks like a domino, especially from the southern end; inside it is long and thin like a train carriage. Its three linked bars, one stone-flagged, are low-beamed, cosy and welcoming. The food is obviously aimed at walkers and hikers. The Ullswater trout, with parsley butter, almonds and home-made tartare sauce, is guaranteed fresh, and the Lion Pot special - a pork casserole - will fill the biggest of gaps.

WHERE TO STAY

Bampton

🏠 ⚥ 🐴 ✉ £

St Patrick's Well Inn, *Bampton, Penrith, Cumbria CA10 2RQ*
Tel: 093 13 244
Open all year

It may be well tucked away near the north end of Haweswater, but this simple b & b and pub built into the fellside gets very busy with walkers on the nearby coast-to-coast footpath and local campers attracted by the smells of landlord James Wilson's classy home cooking. There are three simple rooms, each with double and single bed, TV and hair-dryer (the bathroom is shared). Downstairs the bar has real Marstons bitter as well as a real coal fire, and the food, served from 6.30pm 'till everyone's fed', is all fresh 'except the frozen scampi'. 'If I don't eat it myself I won't use it, it's as simple as that,' says Scotsman Wilson. His *pièce de résistance* is 'Kentucky' fried chicken, done to his own secret recipe. Open all year.

Haweswater
🏠 ⅋ 🐎 ▭ ££

Haweswater Hotel, *Lakeside Road, Bampton, Penrith, Cumbria CA10 2RP*
Tel: 093 13 235/232
Open all year
Stunning location on the edge of Haweswater, shame about the orange sofas, brown stripey carpets and 'seventies tubular steel. But what it lacks in style and creature comforts (less than half the 16 rooms have en suite bathrooms) the hotel makes up for in cheerfulness and peace (it is the only domestic building in the whole of the valley). The rooms are spartan but clean and there's a residents' lounge with satellite TV - not necessarily a welcome facility in this remote spot. The insignia of Manchester Corporation Waterworks on the cutlery and coffee pots betrays the fact that the hotel was built by Manchester Council at the time of the dam construction in the 1930s to replace the Dun Bull Hotel in the drowned village of Mardale. The Mardale Shepherds' Meet which formerly convened in the Dun Bull now meets here every year in November.

Ullswater
🏠 ⅋ 🚫 £

Grove Foot Farm, *Watermillock, Penrith, Cumbria CA11 0NA*
Tel: 07684 86416
Open Mar-Oct

You may need to draw on the encyclopaedic local knowledge of Dot the Milklady to find this remote farmhouse beyond the northern shore of Ullswater. The easy way is to take the turn off the A592 by the Brackenrigg Hotel signposted Greystoke, then left at a crossroads signposted Sparket, Thackthwaite and Matterdale. Grove Foot is on the left up a driveway, a traditionally built Cumbrian farmhouse in a working farm dating from before 1650. The jokey Mrs Hunter, who went to London once but didn't like it, is so concerned that townies might find it cold she's put electric blankets on all the beds (despite the immersion heaters), and the coal fire in the comfortable lounge is often burning in June. This is a lovely old farmhouse with good views and a convivial host.

Ullswater
🏠 ⅋ ▭ £££

The Old Church Hotel, *Watermillock, Penrith, Cumbria CA11 0JN*
Tel: 07684 86204
Open Apr-Oct
One of the finest of the country house hotels dotted on the shore of Ullswater, The Old Church is off the A592 down a long private drive past a little harbour of boats. The lawns, which stretch to the lakeside, are planted with venerable old Irish yews. There are three classes of room - standard, superior and deluxe - chiefly differentiated by size and view rather than furnishings as all are tastefully done out. It's certainly worth paying extra for rooms overlooking the lawns and lake. Otherwise this superb view is avail-

able from the dining room, where the quality of food justifies its price - a typical dinner might start with grilled goat's cheese, followed by broccoli soup, grilled breast of Magret duck, tropical fruit with Sabayon, and a selection of cheeses. Elegance without stuffiness is the byword of The Old Church, so the lapse of taste in the lounge is surprising: unfortunately there's no volume control on the loud and relentlessly pink decor. The cost per night is for room only - a full English breakfast is a steep £13.50 extra per person.

Ullswater
🏠 ✕ 🏃13 🐟 **££££**

Sharrow Bay Country House Hotel, *Ullswater, Penrith, Cumbria CA10 2LZ*
Tel: 07684 86301/86483
Open Mar-Nov
Since it opened as a hotel in 1949 Sharrow Bay has accumulated a hatful of accolades and is still the yardstick by which other country house hotels measure themselves - and find themselves falling short. Its position - on the more secluded, southern shore of Ullswater - the agglomeration of porcelain and antiques, the understated but classic decor, the cuisine, the traditions such as afternoon tea (which is how Sharrow Bay first came to prominence) and the attentiveness of staff, all contribute to the effect. But owners Francis Coulson and Brian Sack have managed to create an indefinable air of something else over the years - call it *cachet* if you will, but it works. The bedrooms (not all with en suite bathrooms, surprisingly) are spread among the main hotel, a cottage in the grounds, an Edwardian lodge at the main gates, Bank House a mile down the lake, and a cottage in the village of Tirril four miles away. Wherever you stay Sharrow Bay is guaranteed not to disappoint. (See also Where to Eat).

WHERE TO EAT

Penrith
✕ ▭ **££-£££**

Chataways Bistro, *St Andrew's Churchyard, Penrith*
Tel: 0768 890233
Open for dinner Tues-Sat all year; Sun lunch and dinner June-Sept
Owners Jeff Brades and Sarah Harding (who does the cooking) are refugees from south London and have had to adjust their thinking since they took over Chataways. 'The people up here are a conservative lot, they like a good plate of beef,' says Sarah. 'But there's always a vegetarian dish on the menu.' She changes the menu every month and in addition to staples such as jugged beef marinated in wine and mustard, the menu might include halibut in tomato and cream sauce, lamb satay, and aubergine and bean layer bake. Puddings such as home-made treacle tart and bread and butter pudding in whisky sauce are worth leaving room for. The wine list, including organic wines, is comprehensive - in due course they hope to include reds from Crimea, Russia and Chile - and there's also Theakston's bitter and Stella and Grolsch lagers. The restaurant, next to the churchyard, is elegantly simple, with low beamed ceiling, whitewashed walls and wooden tables and chairs. Last orders for dinner 10pm.

Penrith
✕ ▭ ££

Nunzios, *1 Castlegate, Penrith*
Tel: 0768 66987
Closed Sun and 3 wks Jan
A no-nonsense Italian joint, functional and cheerful, with regulation red and white decor, gingham tablecloths, echoey pop music, and a very good selection of pastas and pizzas. Specials seem rather over-priced in comparison and include very English fare dressed up in Italian names - *Bistecca alla boscaiola* is sirloin steak in red wine sauce - but *Saltimbocca alla romana* (sliced veal with ham in white wine and sage sauce) is typically Roman and delicious. Last orders: lunch 2.30pm; dinner 11pm.

Penrith
✕ ▭ £££

Passepartout, *51 Castlegate, Penrith*
Tel: 0768 65852
Dinner only; closed Sun & 2 wks Nov
Peter and Rosalind Robinson inherited the name of the restaurant when they took it over, but it is an apt one - they'd worked all over Britain before settling down in this complex of 18th-century farm buildings some six years ago. The restaurant is small and confined to a room at the front, though there's a delightful sun terrace at the back for summer evenings. This will be your only chance to smoke as the dining area is strictly no smoking. Peter's cooking is simply among the best in the Lake District - lots of fish such as salmon, lobster, fish Breton (young turbot and monkfish with tomato and prawns) and seafood au gratin; haunch of venison and Herdwick lamb; vegetarian specials such as ravioli napolitani; wickedly rich puddings (brandy snaps with honey, apricot and whipped cream, hot cherry meringue). The blue Stilton is also unfailingly excellent; and the service is always with a smile. Last orders for dinner 9.30pm.

Ullswater
🏠 ✕ 🖂 ££££

Sharrow Bay Country House Hotel,
Ullswater, Penrith
Tel: 07684 86301/86483
Open Mar-Nov
The restaurant at Sharrow Bay deserves a separate entry not just for the consistently high quality of the food and preparation but because dinner there is an Event orchestrated by four head chefs assisted by their 'Team of Six' , two *pâtissiers* and a master *sommelier*. By tradition the sweet trolley is displayed to diners before they take their seats in the dining room overlooking the lake, and a crash course in speed-reading would be handy to tackle the dauntingly long and detailed menu and wine lists (there are two) for the six courses. The food is mostly traditional English and Scottish: pork, chicken, grouse, salmon, with continental flourishes in the sauces. All in all a consummate mix of quality and style. Open for one sitting only: lunch 1-1.30pm; dinner 8-8.30pm; also afternoon tea 4-4.45pm.

DERWENTWATER

—

Victorian egghead and professional misanthrope John Ruskin was weaned on the beauty of Derwentwater. He was brought to the lakeside when he was an infant and never forgot it; 20 years later when they built the railway to Keswick he was appalled at the notion of the rest of England enjoying it too. Fortunately its charms are inviolable. Derwentwater and Keswick, which stretches to its shore, make a contrasting but happy couple - the lake shapely and bonny and adorned with fells and valleys, the town grey and workaday, but with surprising eccentricities. Between them they'll easily keep you entertained for a day, whatever the weather.

The Derwentwater steamers are the best way of getting round the lake and reaching its sights and vantage points without becoming caught up in traffic. On the western shore there are low level rambles and more taxing hikes; on the east, the Lodore Falls immortalised in the onomatopoeia of Robert Southey's cascading verse, and the hanging valley of Watendlath. From Keswick there is a glorious walk that will take you less than a morning. And if the weather is unkind, the town has some intriguing attractions such as the Cars of the Stars Museum and the tropical swimming pool. There are two lovely drives - Borrowdale to the south of the lake, and through St John's in the Vale to Thirlmere via a stone circle that does for prehistoric rubble what the Sistine Chapel did for ceilings.

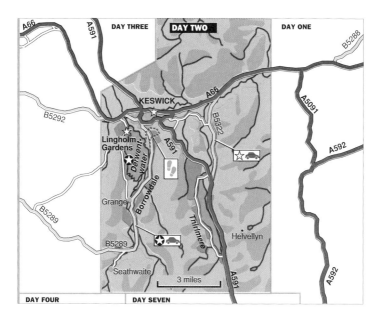

DAY THREE   **DAY TWO**   DAY ONE

KESWICK

Lingholm Gardens

Derwentwater

Borrowdale

Grange

Thirlmere

Helvellyn

B5292

B5289

B5289

Seathwaite

3 miles

DAY FOUR   DAY SEVEN

 ## ✪ BORROWDALE DRIVE

This cracking little valley below Derwentwater runs alongside the shallow-flowing River Derwent and backs into the highest concentration of fells in England, which makes it excellent walking country. But Borrowdale is also a delight for car-bound travellers whose idea of exertion is re-folding an Ordnance Survey map. The B5289 from Keswick takes you down past Derwentwater and into the heart of the valley, following the course of the Derwent as far as Seatoller. The riverbanks are lush, the valley planted with broad-leaved trees that ration the light, dappling the rocky outcrops and mossy boulders - and if all that sounds suspiciously like a romantic painting, well that's what Borrowdale looks like.

A geological freak called the **Bowder Stone**, between the turn-off for Grange village and the village of Rosthwaite, is worth ten minutes of your time on the way down the valley. The car park is well-marked on a curve of the road and the stone itself is five minutes' walk away. The Bowder Stone is a massive boulder, 60 feet long and 35 feet high, dumped here by a passing glacier. Its appeal is not just its bulk but the fact that by some whim of gravity and optical fancy it appears to be precariously balanced on one edge. As you climb the wooden steps to the top it's hard not to worry that you might upset it, even though it's been here a good few million years. The cleft of rock at the top can be slippery so watch your footing. From the top there are views across a standing stone and the road down to the river.

River Derwent, Borrowdale

☀ It's advisable to pack the waterproofs for the next port of call. **Seathwaite** is a straggle of car park and farm buildings reached by a left turn just before Seatoller. Huddled in the valley leading to Glaramara, Great End and Great Gable, it is the wettest inhabited place in Britain (131 inches of rain a year, compared to 57 inches for Keswick just 12 miles to the north) on account of being first in the firing line when moist westerly air rises over the mountain peaks and cools and condenses to form clouds. This is serious walkers' country but there's also a gentle flat stroll along the valley floor that will give you the peace of the fells without the pain.

Park before the farm buildings and follow the path through them. The farmer here is particularly hot on dogs who worry sheep (he posts up a notice of how many dogs he's killed recent-ly), so if you have a dog make sure it's under control, preferably on the lead if it's lambing season. Continue on the path along-side Grain's Gill. A waterfall, Taylor Gill Force, becomes visible on your right, though it's no great shakes from this distance. A lovely little bridge called **Stockley Bridge** is a sensible goal - after that the path rises to join the gruelling Styhead Pass flank-ing Great Gable before descending into Wasdale. The grassy banks of the gill by the bridge are a good place to pause and con-template the masochists toiling up towards Styhead.

There are remains of old graphite or 'wadd' mines (used for the manufacture of pencils in Keswick) on the fellside above the farm at Seathwaite. Take the path from the farm past the camp-site if you're interested, but some of the old shafts are dangerous and apparently not very interesting either.

Seatoller marks the western extremity of Borrowdale. From here the road climbs steeply to reach Buttermere via the Honister Pass. Opposite the Yew Tree restaurant (park in the National Trust car park just before the bend) the **Seatoller Barn Information Centre**, run by the Lake District National Park Authority, has a permanent exhibition of the history, geology, plants and wildlife of Borrowdale.

Seatoller Barn Information Centre, Dalehead Base, Borrowdale. Tel: 07687 77294
Opening times: daily Easter-end Sept 10am-5pm
On Sats there are craft skills courses such as 'Drawing from observation' and 'Creative corn dollies' bookable in advance from The Events Office, Brockhole National Park Visitor Centre, Windermere LA23 1LJ (tel: 05394 46601)

Back up the B5289 right in the Jaws of Borrowdale (as the valley entrance is known) **Grange Bridge Cottage** is an exquisite place for lunch or perhaps an early dinner. Situated on the left over the stone bridge, this traditional flint-built cottage used to be the village shop and post office. Ron and Joan Norey have built a reputation for home-baked afternoon teas but their hot meals, served all day, are delicious too. You won't go wrong with grilled Seathwaite trout (from the fish farm there) or steak and kidney pudding, and there's a good selection of sandwiches, sa-lads, ploughman's and baked potatoes. Grange Bridge Cottage is open April 1-end Oct 11.30am-7pm; April-June closed Mondays; February-March weekends only.

✪   DERWENTWATER

The fattest of the lakes, dotted with islands, accessible all round by car and with some lovely lakeshore paths, Derwentwater is a beauty. The most popular route for motorists is the eastern shore road, the B5289, down into Borrowdale. This meets the more remote western shore road at Grange. Both roads have stopping places and vantage points, but the western side of the lake has the most accessible walking. Brandelhow Park, the very first National Trust property, has woodland trails along the shore, and the ridge-backed mountain called Cat Bells that dominates this side of the lake has various access points, the easiest probably being between Brandelhow and Swinside (there's a car park there).

Ashness Bridge, with Derwentwater, Keswick and Skiddaw

Watendlath Beck

Back on the east side, the fork signposted to **Ashness Bridge** and **Watendlath** is a delightful meandering little dead-end that gets dreadfully clogged in summer. It leads to the hamlet of Watendlath where there's a car park, a scattering of buildings, a café and a tarn. But most people are drawn by the prospect of setting eyes on a view they've seen a thousand times before on calendars and postcards - Ashness Bridge just up from the shore road, with its panorama of Derwentwater behind. Beyond it there's a car park and vantage point called Surprise View - don't go too near the edge - and a recommended walk in Ashness Wood. Follow the track marked 'Permissive footpath to Watendlath' . At the bottom cross a wooden ladder gate, followed by a bridge over the beck, then follow signs to Lodore. When you reach the beck that feeds the falls, follow it until you reach a high vantage point with the falls rushing below a sheer drop.

The more popular way to view **Lodore Falls** is round the back of the Swiss Lodore Hotel on the B5289, though parking is a problem. Just south of the main entrance to the hotel there's a lay-by by a public lavatory: parking is allowed only for those using the loo, but you can just about see the falls in the time it would take to powder your nose. Follow the road round behind the hotel. It takes you over a bridge and in two minutes you are by the falls. There's a 5p honesty box set in the hotel wall. The falls can disappoint if it has not rained recently. In any case they are not the Lakes' most exciting waterfalls - their greatest claim to fame is being written about by Robert Southey in his poem *How the Falls come down at Lodore*.

The wooden Edwardian pleasure cruisers, *Lady Windermere* and *Margaret Rose*, that ply Derwentwater both clockwise and anti-clockwise are a good alternative for getting around the lake. Apart from the terminus at Keswick there are six landing stages: Nichol End Marine at the north-west corner which is a sailing and windsurfing centre; Hawes End for access to Cat Bells; Low and High Brandelhow for good shore-side walks; Lodore for the falls and Borrowdale; and Ashness Gate for the bridge and Watendalth. Or you can do a round trip which takes 50 minutes.

Information from the Keswick on Derwentwater Launch Co Ltd, 29 Manor Park, Keswick (tel: 07687 72263)

There are regular sailings all day, starting at 10am in season (from end Mar-3rd Sun in Nov) rising to 20 or more a day subject to demand; off season there are 4 scheduled sailings on weekends only (10.30am, 11.30am, 1.30pm, 2.30pm). Evening cruises take place from Spring Bank Hol-Sept 15, leaving at 8.30pm until Aug 31 and 7.30pm thereafter

Prices: adult £3 in winter, £3.85 in summer; child £1 in winter, £1.90 in summer; family ticket for 5 £6 in winter, £8.50 in summer

In season there are motorboats for hire (£8 an hour for 2 people) and rowing boats (adult £2.50 an hour, child £1.25)

DERWENTWATER WALK

From the landing stages at Lakeside there is an excellent 2½ mile walk (it should take you a leisurely hour and a half) that takes in just about the best that Derwentwater has to offer without requiring you to break into a sweat. Follow the shoreline (or the procession of people, take your pick) to a rocky promontory, planted with Scots pines, known as **Friar's Crag**. The view from here is another one of Lakeland's visual cliches. John Ruskin reckoned it one of the very best views in Europe. That may be pushing it a bit but it is certainly startlingly expansive given the lowly elevation; it is perhaps something to do with the naturally pleasing composition, with the pines framing the water and the islands - Lord's and St Herbert's - imaging the gentle bulks of the fells in the background.

Derwentwater from Friar's Crag

Loop back from the viewing point, turn right behind the memorial to Ruskin and pass through a gate on to the flat grassy foreshore. Just before a footbridge turn left behind a tree and, keeping the church spire in your sights, pass into a wood. At a junction of paths take the right turn. Cross the road (B5289) and turn immediately left parallel to it. After a while go right up a steep path that turns at right angles to take you to the summit of Castlehead. Take care underfoot - the rocks up here can be very slippery. There's a cairn of rocks with a viewing disc pointing out Skiddaw, Scafell Pike, Blencathra and other summits but it is the views of Derwentwater that make the ascent worthwhile.

Return by the same path but then instead of turning left back to the road follow the path straight ahead that runs parallel to a wire fence. Cross a field and turn left in front of some houses. Left again and you're in Ambleside Road. Opposite Church Street take the footpath between St John's Church and the school, past the Royal Air Force Association Club. At Borrowdale Road turn left, then right on to another footpath that leads to Lake Road. Turn left and back to the car park near the landing stages.

☆ ## KESWICK

Keswick, 'Birthplace of the Pencil', has a fine natural setting - in the shadow of Skiddaw and on the shore of Derwentwater - which its streets of grey slate houses can't quite live up to. But it's a friendly - and user-friendly - place with good parking facilities off Heads Road and round the back of Market Place and a reasonably compact shopping centre. The well-staffed **Tourist Information Centre** (tel: 07687 72645) in Moot Hall on Market Place - one of Keswick's few notable buildings - is open all year.

Keswick has some eccentric attractions to keep you off the streets when it rains. The **Cars of the Stars Motor Museum** has the same kind of appeal as the train set in the attic - the kids may drag you there but it'll be the dads who enjoy it most, especially as many of the vehicles on display are from films and television series of 'sixties and 'seventies vintage. They include Simon Templar's white Volvo from *The Saint*, Chitty Chitty Bang Bang, Knightrider's supercar (called 'Kitt' for some reason), Bergerac's burgundy Triumph roadster, and Del Boy's Reliant Regal Supervan (complete with furry dice and scrawled notice on the windscreen saying 'Tax in post') from *Only Fools and Horses*. These are the actual vehicles used in filming, though some others (James Dean's Porsche is the most glaring example) are reconstructions. All are presented within rather crude film-sets, but however much you want to sneer it's all good clean fun - besides, Emma Peel's Lotus Elan is there, and who could wish for more?

Cars of the Stars Motor Museum, Standish Street, Keswick. Tel: 07687 73757
Opening times: daily 2 wks before Easter–end Oct 10am–5pm
Admission: adult £1.80; child £1.20

Too many of the Lake District's museums and exhibitions are now given over to computerised gizmos geared for people with the attention span of plankton, so it's refreshing to find a truly old-fashioned Victorian museum. As the blurb for the **Keswick Museum and Art Gallery** says: 'The atmosphere and Victorian flavour contribute to a more satisfying and genuine experience which is bypassed by the push-button plastic era.' It was built in 1897 and claims to be the only purpose-built Victorian museum still in existence. Many of its delights have to be rootled out. The mummified 500-year-old cat found in the rafters of a church is hidden in a trunk where it luxuriates bizarrely in a velvet-lined glass box; the Victorian collection of butterflies, moths and sundry bugs is tucked away in sliding drawers - some of the moths are plump as small birds, others as delicate as the tiniest meadow flowers. There are other oddities such as the musical stones, arranged like a stone-age keyboard, the tree root growing over a horseshoe, and Flintoft's Model of the Lake District, which took one Joseph Flintoft 17 years to complete and was first exhibited in 1834. The art gallery is disappointing. There are a few original manuscripts from Southey, Wordsworth and Walpole, but the paintings are part of a changing exhibition by local artists and pretty dreadful on the whole. One shining exception is the work of 19th-century amateur artist Joseph Brown Junior. His 'Skaters on Derwentwater', done in 1870, puts Lowry to shame.

Keswick Museum and Art Gallery, Fitz Park, Station Road, Keswick. Tel: 07687 73263
Opening times: Good Fri-Oct 31 10am-noon, 1-4pm (closed Sat)
Admission: adult 80p; child 40p

 Keswick Leisure Pool is a polygonal re-creation of a tropical climate with palm fronds, sun umbrellas, a gently sloping water's edge that forms a ceramic beach - and a fast food outlet. It has an ambient air temperature of 30°C, water temperature of 84°F and 'ozone disinfection' so it doesn't smell of chlorine. The depth of the water goes from zero to just 1.6 metres, so you won't run the gauntlet of skydiving lunatics, and there's a wonderful blue tubular water slide called a flume.

Keswick Leisure Pool, Station Road, Keswick. Tel: 07687 72760
Opening times: Oct 31-Mar 31, Mon-Fri 10am-5pm, closed Sat & Sun; Apr 1-June 1
& Oct, Wednes-Fri 1pm-6pm, Sat & Sun 10am-5pm; June & Sept daily 10am-6pm;
Jul & Aug Mon-Fri 10am-8pm, Sat & Sun 10am-6pm
Admission: adult £2.50; child under 18 £2; family ticket for 5 £7.50

Laurel and Hardy's Model T Ford in the Cars of the Stars Motor Museum

Keswick has several good places for lunch. One of the best is **Abraham's Tea Room** at the top of the George Fisher leisure store in Borrowdale Road. You pass through floors of Barbour and Goretex to reach the restaurant perched under the rafters. It is light and airy and strictly no smoking. Filtered water is used for the tea and coffee and the coffee beans are freshly ground. The open sandwiches, such as local baked ham with peach and smoked turkey with port jelly, are meals in themselves but if you feel like going to town try the chicken, ham and chestnut pie. Do leave room for some home baking: Applethwaite shortcake, gooey chocolate fingers or caramel and walnut shorties. This is a good place for rendezvous as there's a noticeboard for leaving messages. The tea room is open every day all year round and hot food is served all day.

There are only so many things you can say about a stick of lead, but the **Pencil Museum** tries its best. The world's first pencil was made in Keswick in 1558. The Cumberland Pencil Company, purveyor of quality pencils to the entire world, has been here since the 1830s when the graphite used for the pencil core was mined at Borrowdale (this source was commercially exhausted by 1900 and the graphite is now imported). It is still the major employer in Keswick, tourism apart, though it has kept abreast of the times by diversifing into staplers and binders. The museum has a reconstruction of a graphite, or 'plumbago', mine which is safer than visiting the real thing above Seathwaite, and lots and lots of pencils including The Longest Pencil in the World. The collection of wartime pencils is pretty exciting, as pencils go: these were manufactured under strict secrecy and issued to Bomber Command crews and sent in Red Cross parcels to PoWs. The metal tip containing an eraser could be unscrewed to reveal a tiny compass on the underside and in the empty pencil casing was a tiny furled map of Germany with marked escape routes. All very James Bond - but this was for real.

The Pencil Museum, The Cumberland Pencil Co Ltd, Southey Works, Greta Bridge, Keswick. Tel: 07687 73626
Opening times: daily 9.30am-4pm
Admission: adult £1.50; child 75p

LINGHOLM GARDENS

The gardens attached to Lingholm House, where Beatrix Potter wrote *Squirrel Nutkin*, have a marvellous collection of rhododendrons and azaleas so the best time to visit is late spring (April-May), though some flower as early as February. The gardens are informally laid out among meandering paths and there are lots of other interesting trees and shrubs, explained in an informative free leaflet. The only hazard is possible back-strain from bending low to read the species names planted at ground level, and the only regret the fact that the nearby shore of Derwentwater, where Squirrel Nutkin rafted across the lake, is not included in the walk. There's a tea room selling scones, cakes and sandwiches, and seeds from the garden. The greenhouse behind it sells begonias, blue poppies, geraniums, ferns, gentians and primula.

Lingholm Gardens are a mile south of Portinscale on the road to Grange.
Tel: 07687 72003
Opening times: daily Apr 1-Oct 31 10am-5pm
Admission: adult £2.20; child under 16 free. No dogs

THIRLMERE DRIVE

 Thirlmere is one of the forgotten puddles of Cumbria - it's easy to get blasé about so many stunning stretches of water - but the history of the valley is interesting. There is a route to it round the back roads from Keswick with a couple of highlights along the way that make it a rewarding excursion.

Castlerigg Stone Circle

Take the un-numbered road off the link road between the A591 and the A66 on the eastern outskirts of Keswick. This takes you to **Castlerigg Stone Circle**, a circle of 38 Bronze Age stones (with a further 10 forming an enclosure) 100 feet in diameter on a low flat-topped hill which is always accessible. It is particularly memorable for its setting: the site enclosed by a magnificent sweep of fells that echoes the configuration of the stones themselves, stones and mountains forming concentric circles many miles apart. To the north are Skiddaw and Blencathra, to the south the craggy outlines of High Rigg and the Helvellyn range, to the west the Derwent fells. We'll never know what Castlerigg was for, but whether it was an astronomical observatory, a place of sacrifice or simply a place to meet and chew the fat, the people who built it knew what they were doing. To experience Castlerigg at its most atmospheric, as well as to avoid the photographers, frisbee players and picnickers, visit early in the morning or at dusk when if you're lucky the rising or setting sun plays miraculous tricks on the fellsides all around.

Continue along the road, turning right at successive junctions. This will bring you on to the B5322 running along **St John's in** the Vale, an unspoilt little valley that is ignored by visitors for the most part, probably because it doesn't really go anywhere and there is nowhere to eat or drink. Still, their loss will be your gain. The valley is flat-bottomed and vividly green, contrasting with the forbidding steep slopes on the eastern side (the last gasp of the Helvellyn range) and the gentler contours of High and Low Rigg to the west. It is sparsely populated, dotted with whitewashed farms, and there's a cricket green with a pavilion improvised from a green-painted railway carriage. Its best known feature is a crag down at the southern end called Castle Rock, towering above two tall, freshly painted cottages. As the road joins the A591 at Legburthwaite, it is worth looking back at the valley's formidable natural entrance of craggy jaws.

St John's in the Vale, looking south to Castle Rock

To reach **Thirlmere** turn right on to the A591 and then immediately left. Thirlmere, like Haweswater, is now a reservoir and it is salutary to consider how utterly man can change a landscape in so short a time. The reservoir was created in 1894 to supply Manchester. Before that there were two small lakes in the valley, Leathes Water and Wythburn Water, a few houses and the palatial Armboth House. Wordsworth and Coleridge would leave their respective homes in Grasmere and Keswick and meet up here for poetical trysts - a rock bearing their carved initials was blown up before the flooding and now lies in a shattered heap in the garden of Dove Cottage. Remains of walls and tree-stumps are sometimes visible when the water level drops.

Thirlmere is owned by the North-West Water Authority and was closed to the public until ten years ago, when improvements in water treatment eliminated the risk of pollution. It is still not exactly welcoming. The road crosses the dam at the northern end of the reservoir and follows the line of its western shore, rejoining the A591 beyond its southern tip. From Armboth car park you can follow the shoreline south, but it is hard going underfoot. Further south there are forest trails, and at Dobgill car park there's a waymarked path to Harrop Tarn. There are more forest trails on the east side by the A591. Otherwise, it is a challenging exercise to just sit and imagine the valley as it must have been.

Swimming and motor boats are banned. Fishing is free to holders of rod licences, available for £12.50 from The National Rivers Authority, PO Box 12, Richard Fairclough House, Knutsford,Warrington WA4 1HG; tel: 0925 53999

WHERE TO STAY

Borrowdale

☖ ☂ ▭ £

Derwent House, *Grange in Borrowdale, Keswick, Cumbria CA12 5UY*
Tel: 07687 77658
Closed Christmas & Jan
Every window has a breathtaking view in this slate-built guesthouse on the banks of the River Derwent. Take your pick from Grange Fell, High Spy, Skiddaw, Cat Bells, Maiden Moor, or the rambling orchard garden on the riverside. Derwent House is on a curve of the B5289 south of the turning for Grange, right in the heart of Borrowdale. There's free fishing from the end of the garden. Rooms are simple and cosy, most with attached bathrooms and all with TV. Breakfasts, which cost extra, are taken in a light stone-flagged room and there are optional evening meals every day at 7pm except Sunday, cooked by owner Deirdre Lopez using fresh local produce. A typical menu might include roast leg of lamb with rosemary or rib of local beef, followed by apple and mincemeat crumble or strawberries and cream.

Borrowdale

☖ ☂ ✉ ££

Greenbank, *Borrowdale, Keswick, Cumbria CA12 5UJ*
Tel: 07687 77215
Closed Dec
In the words of one regular guest: 'a lovely homely place, and excellent food'. Greenbank is tucked on a shelf of fellside at the end of a long climbing drive off the B5289. In the 12 years they've been here, Trevor and Jennifer Lorton have created a discreet and classy little place that is very good value for money. It is lighter and airier than many small hotels, with Monet prints on the walls, pretty floral wallpaper and expansive views of Borrowdale and Derwentwater. The best place to see the lake is from the bath in one of the 'superior' rooms on the north side.

All the rooms are tasteful and comfortable, and though you'll pay more for views of Derwentwater, the scenery is spectacular wherever you sleep. There are two lounges, both with log fires and one with TV, and a gong summons guests to dinner in the licensed dining room at 7pm. The four-course meals are a cut above the usual - typically, smoked trout salad, breast of chicken with Stilton and celery stuffing, strawberry tart, and cheeseboard.

Keswick

⌂ ⅓12 ▬ ££££

Underscar Manor, *Applethwaite, nr Keswick, Cumbria CA12 4PH*
Tel: 07687 75000
Open all year

The architecture of this former retreat of a Liverpool cotton tycoon is officially described as Italianate - which just means it's sunnier and more frivolous than your average grim Victorian pile. And well it may be, for if you were a house you could not wish for a more idyllic spot to put down your foundations. Underscar Manor is set in 40 acres of gardens and woodland on the foothills of Skiddaw, with views of Derwentwater and the fells beyond that for once earn the adjective panoramic. It's been open only two years but in that time owners Pauline and Derek Harrison and Gordon Evans have built a reputation for elegance, quality and fine food. It's not cheap, but there's a sliding scale for rooms, all of them tastefully furnished in different styles. Room 3, which has a balcony and the best view, is sheer opulence, but everyone

has the benefit of the food and view in the conservatory restaurant, where first and main courses might include char-grilled goose breast with duck confit and wild mushrooms, or fillet of beef with stuffed oxtail, glazed shallots and a Madeira sauce. There's also the option of the 'Menu Surprise' when each of the six surprise courses is described as it is served.

Newlands

⌂ ⅓12 ✉ £££

Swinside Lodge Hotel, *Newlands, Keswick, Cumbria CA12 5UE*
Tel: 07687 72948
Closed Dec - mid-Feb

The shore of Derwentwater is five minutes away, Catbells is in the back garden and the lovely Newlands Valley is just round the corner. Swinside Lodge, a Victorian house set in gardens of beech, willow, sycamore and lilac, equals luxurious living at affordable prices. The nine rooms are individually decorated - the attic room with sloping ceiling is worth asking specially for - but the highlight is the five-course evening menu which changes daily. As owner Graham Taylor says - truthfully if immodestly - 'You'll not get better food for this price anywhere in the Lake District'. Starters might be chicken and spinach pancake or mushroom tart, followed by soup and poached salmon, rounded off with sticky toffee pudding and cheese. The dining room is candlelit, and though it's not licensed you can bring your own wine.

WHERE TO EAT

Borrowdale
× ⚔ ▭ £££

The Yew Tree, *Seatoller, Borrowdale, Keswick*
Tel: 07687 77634
Closed from early Jan for a month, Mon all day & Fri lunch

There's no other word for it - the 17th-century cottages that comprise the Yew Tree really do 'nestle' at the foot of the Honister Pass. These are just about the oldest buildings in Borrowdale, dating from 1628, and the slate floors and oak beams are certainly charming, even if the decor is best described as rustic kitsch. Still, the food is absolutely delicious and the staff - a heavy contingent from Down Under - cheerful and unstuffy. Most of the food grew up within a stone's throw and the freshness tells. The staples are steak, trout, salmon and duck, and the specials - try the rack of lamb if it's on - sublime. For those who prefer the local wildlife to be running about rather than on a plate, there are three vegetarian dishes a day and there's a lighter lunch menu. Last orders: lunch 2pm; dinner 9pm (earlier on Sunday).

Keswick
📧 ✉ £

Dog & Gun, *2 Lake Road, Keswick*
Tel: 07687 73463
Open all year

This unpretentious town-centre pub has built up a loyal clientele through word of mouth, especially among walkers and climbers. Its hearty menu is best appreciated after a day's walking, though even the biggest of appetites may be unequal to the speciality of the house. The Hungarian goulash is a legacy of a previous landlord and comes with spuds, dumplings and a hunk of garlic granary bread, so don't order a starter. There's a good salad selection and tasty 'fillers' such as Cumberland sausage and onions in a brown roll, and the beer - Theakston's - is good too. The bar tends to get congested - try for a seat in the stone-flagged area up by the open fire - and the music is strictly for thirty-something nostalgics. Last orders: lunch 2pm; dinner 9.30pm.

Keswick
× ✉ ££

Mayson's, *Lake Road, Keswick*
Tel: 07687 74104
Open 10am-9pm Easter-Whitsun & 2nd wk Jul-Nov 1; 10am-4.30pm at other times

This unusual cross between a café and a bistro offers what appears to be a contradiction in terms: fast, not to say lightning quick, food that is also fresh, home-made (including the bread) and delicious. The secret is the self-service system that enables you to choose from a wide and exotic selection of hot meals, posted on a blackboard, that are then microwaved in the time it takes to pay the bill. These might include Indonesian vegetable curry, spicy mushroom rissoles, and Cajun chicken kebabs rustled up fresh every day by owner and chef Richard Bainbridge. There's a good choice of drinks too, from trendy beers like Rolling Rock to cheap carafes of wine. The large windows, skylight, stripped pine and hanging plants lend the place a casual, slightly 'alternative' air.

NORTH - WESTERN LAKES

This sweep of the National Park involves a fair bit of motoring between points of interest, from Bassenthwaite Lake round to remote and inhospitable Ennerdale Water. In between there is Cockermouth - pleasant if unremarkable, and the only place of any size - and the exquisite chain of lakes of which Buttermere is the jewel.

'Conquering' Skiddaw, one of the very highest of the Lake District fells, will take you a good morning. The summit of Dodd, further up by Bassenthwaite Lake, is a shorter alternative, and the walks and adventure playgrounds in the gardens of Mirehouse are a gradient-free way of letting off energy. But even if you are not a keen walker, make time for the circuit of Buttermere, one of the easiest and finest walks in the Lakes.

Understanding and enjoying nature is very much the theme of the Whinlatter Pass Visitor Centre, where children can lose themselves for hours among the waymarked trails. The weather is always an imponderable of course, and should it close in with a vengeance Cockermouth will see you right - though the tour of Jennings brewery will hardly keep you dry. Or just drive and look - there's little in the way of man-made attractions, but nature herself, especially in the haughty magnificence of the fells around Buttermere and Crummock Water, is spellbinding enough.

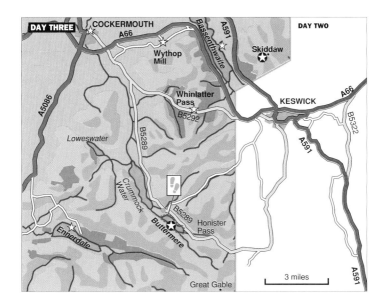

 ☆ BASSENTHWAITE LAKE

Bassenthwaite Lake itself is a bit of a dud, not to mince words. The ingredients are there - the lowering presence of Skiddaw to the east, panoramic views from Whinlatter Pass to the west - but somehow they don't add up, partly because the western shore is completely spoilt by the A66 to Cockermouth and Workington.

The best way of taking in the lake is via the eastern shore on the A591 to Carlisle. There's an excellent cluster of attractions up here, centred around the car park at **Dodd Wood**. Dodd Wood is owned by the Forestry Commission. There are four trails of differing lengths which are clearly colour-coded, but the logging which still goes on doesn't make for good walking terrain - the tractors churn up the paths and some of the denuded tracts of fellside are extremely unattractive, like plucked poultry. Still, it's worth slogging to the 1,600ft summit of Dodd. Stretching below, the alluvial plain between Bassenthwaite and Derwentwater clearly shows how the two lakes were once joined.

Dodd Wood is always accessible. A very informative Forestry Commision leaflet, containing maps of the trails and diagrams of the views from the summit, is available for 50p from the Old Sawmill in the car park

The **Old Sawmill Tearoom** has a limited but appetising menu - soup and roll, sandwiches, salads and jacket potatoes, or, appropriately enough, Woodman's Lunch: two cheeses, French bread, salad and choice of pickle. As well as the usual hot and cold drinks, Ovaltine and Bournevita are available, which are just the job after trudging calf-deep through viscous mud. The fire engine on show here had its moment of glory in 1887 when a hot air balloon crashed on Dodd and started a forest fire.

The Old Sawmill is also where you buy tickets for **Mirehouse** and grounds on the other side of the A591. Mirehouse is the seat of the Spedding family who were well in with people like Wordsworth and Tennyson. The central part of the house was built in 1666; the Speddings took it over in 1802 and the family has lived here ever since. Now they live above the shop, as it

St Bega's Church, Bassenthwaite Lake

were, as the downstairs has been open to the public on two afternoons a week since 1981.

Mirehouse may be steeped in literary associations but it is far from being bookish and sepulchral as such places often are. Current owner John Spedding is a delightful cove who describes the house as 'a homely sort of place' and says he hates 'the funereal reverence some people bring to it'. To prove a point, Mr Spedding is big on noise - both the formal variety (a pianist plays during opening hours) and the cacophonous (the bell system for summoning servants, the dinner gong, a barrel organ). Children are particularly welcome - a Junior Visitors' Guide and Quiz is available for 5p and there are games to play like Hunt the Commode and Find the Secret Drawer. Meanwhile bibliophiles can hunt down a first edition of Dr Johnson's Dictionary of 1755, in four volumes.

In the grounds there are four adventure playgrounds including a mini-orienteering course, rope bridges over a beck, swings and a 'castle' made from wooden palings. There are also lovely walks by the lakeshore, where Tennyson wrote the Excalibur bit of *Morte d'Arthur*. Bassenthwaite will never look better than from here - or from the path to the frail and spiritual little church of **St Bega** which is pre-Norman with evidence of even earlier building in its walls.

Mirehouse is on the A591 five miles north of Keswick
Opening times: Apr-Oct Sun, Wednes & Bank Hol Mons 2-5pm; grounds and Old Sawmill Tearoom daily Apr-Oct 10.30am-5.30pm
Admission: house and grounds - adult £2.40; child £1.20; grounds only - adult 80p; child 60p

 ## BUTTERMERE

 There's a limpid simplicity about Buttermere that is unequalled by any other of the lakes. Intimidated as it is by the robustly named peaks of High Crag, High Stile and Red Pike to the southwest, the Buttermere Fells on the other side and Fleetwith Pike at its head, it still steals the show. The approach on the B5289, over the Honister Pass from Borrowdale, is the best way to set eyes on it. The same road from the other direction, down the Vale of Lorton from Cockermouth, is also pretty special.

Honister Pass

LAKESHORE WALK

Buttermere is a nicely proportioned lake, almost rectangular, of just over a mile in length and with enough width to reflect film-like images of the fells in its celluloid waters. The anti-clockwise walk round it is likewise joyfully simple. Park in Buttermere 'village' - a one-horse town if ever there was one - near the Fish Inn (the Maid of Buttermere, written about by Melvyn Bragg among others, was daughter of the innkeeper here). Take the path to the left of the inn. If you're interested in a four-mile detour to one of Lakeland's highest waterfalls (of disputed height, but somewhere around 130 feet) take the footpath off to the right signposted Scale Force. Otherwise the path you're on will take you across two footbridges to the edge of the lake, where you just keep going.

Through Burntness Wood there are views of Fleetwith Pike towering over Honister Pass. The path passes beyond the end of the lake, through Gatesgarth Farm, and on to the B5289. Turn left and walk by the road for 300 yards before cutting back on to the lakeshore. A little further along, where the shore juts, is a viewpoint called Shingle Point looking across to High Crag and High Stile. Beyond it the path passes through a quarried tunnel which looks longer than it really is, before passing through a farmyard, past the Bridge Inn, and back to the car park.

Buttermere is the best known of a chain of lakes also including Crummock Water and Loweswater. These two tend to suffer in comparison with Buttermere - if they were sited anywhere else their praises would be hymned much more volubly than they are. **Crummock Water** is Buttermere's much larger Siamese twin. The delta of land between them was once underwater and they are still umbilically joined by a brook. It is possible to make a circuit of Crummock on foot - parking is on the B5289 a little over halfway up from Buttermere, or just off the road to Loweswater - and the shingle beaches on the western side are a pleasure to walk. But it is boggy, hard-going in places, and long - nearly nine miles - and besides, its qualities are just as well appreciated from a car. The striking thing about Crummock Water is the angular fells that surround it - on the east side above the road the crags of Rannerdale Knotts, to the north-east Grasmoor and Whiteside, to the west the sheer, intimidating, ridge of Mellbreak.

This is wild country. A couple of miles to the north-west (you have to double back off the B5289) **Loweswater** is a pussycat by comparison. It has the misfortune to suffer from a painful sounding problem with its waterworks: it is the only lake in the Lake District whose waters flow in (that is, eastwards) - into Crummock Water - instead of west to the sea. It is small, has a farmhouse at its southern end showing very white against the

Buttermere looking towards Fleetwith Pike

green fields, and it looks hopelessly cowed beneath the thuggish gable end of Mellbreak. But never fear - it is protected by the National Trust. Walking round it is a doddle. The problem is that the north-eastern shore has to be walked largely by road if the water level is high.

No motorboats are allowed on any of the three lakes; small yachts and rowing boats are allowed on Buttermere and Crummock. Rowing boats for hire on Buttermere are available from Mrs Richardson, Gatesgarth Farm, Buttermere (tel: 07687 70256): £3 per hour, £8 for half a day, £12 for a full day. Rowing boats for Crummock Water can be hired from Mrs Beard of Rannerdale Farm, Buttermere (07687 70232) at a similar cost.

Loweswater

☆ COCKERMOUTH

Like Penrith, this small market town is just outside the National Park boundary, which loops inward to avoid it. Thus excused from participating in the tourist jamboree, Cockermouth gets on quietly with its business - except on Friday and Saturday nights when the local youth, fuelled on a potent cocktail of hormones, boredom and drink, paint the town red. Most people come to see the birthplace of its most famous son and daughter, William and Dorothy Wordsworth, but it's worth exploring some of the rest of the town too. A booklet called *Cockermouth: Walks Around the Town*, detailing a four-mile circuit and a shorter town centre walk, is available for 50p from the **Tourist Information Centre** in Riverside car park which is open daily all year; tel: 0900 822634.

> The **Courthouse Antiques and Craft Market** on Main Street, near the bridge, occupies a split level floor at the top of the building, in what was the old court house. In the way of these bric a brac markets it is the expectation of happening on something - a lovely old watercolour, the perfect corner cabinet - that makes a visit worthwhile, and the Courthouse is better stocked than many such places. Open 10am-5pm Monday-Saturday all year; tel: 0900 824346.

The Wordsworth trail starts in earnest at **Wordsworth House,** now owned by the National Trust, though in 1937, before the Trust took it over, it was going to be demolished to make way for a bus station. The house where William and sister Dorothy were born, in 1770 and 1771 respectively, is an imposing Georgian pile, with lots of windows that must have made it a terrific tax liability in its time, which could well be why its owner, the Earl of Lowther, handed it over to the Wordsworths rent-free. The house also has a peach-coloured façade that, incongruously, lends it the air of a French provincial *mairie* - all that's missing is the tricolour hanging above the porch. There are seven rooms open to the public, all furnished in the Regency style.

Wordsworth House, Cockermouth

It has little genuine Wordsworthiana to savour, and none from the Cockermouth years - a sofa and bookcase from Rydal Mount, part of a Crown Derby dinner service, the poet's inkstand, and Dorothy's gilt mirror and tripod table. Otherwise look out for the collection of late 18th- and early 19th-century prints of the Lake District, executed when artists were still grappling with the principles of perspective, and an early Turner of a Welsh castle.

Wordsworth House is on the north side of Main Street towards the bottom end.
Tel: 0900 824805
Opening times: May 1-Oct 31 weekdays 11am-4.30pm; Sun 2-4.30pm; closed Thurs
Admission: adult £2.30; child £1.20; NT members free

It's not recorded whether Wordsworth liked a pint of Jennings but the brewery was certainly in existence while he was still alive. The **Jennings Brewery** is open for guided tours (children have to be over 12) which attempt to demystify the process described by Head Brewer Frank Smith as 'a combination of an exact science, old fashioned cookery and a touch of magic'. It's a good idea to wear flat shoes as the tour involves some gridded walkways.

Jennings is the only independent brewer in Cumbria which is reason enough to drink its beer. It also happens to be good stuff. The water used to produce it is drawn from a Norman well which used to belong to the castle up on the hill (I may have been imagining it, but the resulting brew does seem to taste exceptionally pure). You will probably come out little the wiser on the arcane workings of 'mash tuns', 'wort', 'boiling coppers' and Original and Specific Gravity, but the experience is interesting nevertheless. You feel rather like a dotty boffin as you peer over from one bubbling concoction to the next, and the heady atmosphere - best described as like socks drying on a radiator - ensures you emerge half-cut. The job is completed in the little bar in which you get a free half-pint of either Dark Mild, Original, Cumberland Ale or Sneck Lifter (the latter should only be available on prescription).

Jennings Brothers Brewery is reached by taking High Sand Lane off Main Street (oppo-
site Station Street by the New Bookshop) and crossing the River Cocker just before its
confluence with the Derwent. The brewery shop and tour reception is 100 yards on the
right. Tel: 0900 823214
Tour times: Feb 1-Nov 30, twice daily 10.30am and 2pm Mon-Fri
Admission: adult £2, child £1.50

The **Norham Coffee House and Restaurant** in Main Street offers home cooking at its very finest, albeit in a slightly prim atmosphere. Smoked ham, from the smokery that supplies Fortnum & Mason, is just one of the choices for sandwiches or salads. There's also quiche, ratatouille and omelettes, and a delicious selection of local ice-creams such as Borrowdale Blackcurrant and Scaithwaite Strawberry. Children have their own menu - fish fingers, chicken nuggets, baked beans. And to remind you of what you're missing there's a framed set of dietary tables from the Cockermouth Workhouse hanging on the wall. The Norham is open Monday-Wednesday 9am-5.30pm, Thursday-Saturday 9am-7.30pm, Sunday 12-6pm.

☆ ENNERDALE WATER

This reservoir is probably the remotest of the lakes and whatever the traffic congestion elsewhere Ennerdale Water is guaranteed to be relatively peaceful. It is hardly the most attractive of lakes though, despite the massive peaks at its eastern end. The Forestry Commission's conifer plantations along its north shore are drab and uniform, and the western end is flat and boring; a new water treatment works is being built there at the moment and the area is blighted by a settlement of green site huts and cranes. The contrast between the west and east - the head and feet of the lake's foetal shape - is a graphic illustration of the two main types of rock that make up the Lake District. The craggy fells to the east - Steeple, Pillar and High Stile - are part of the Borrowdale Volcanics; at the other end is the soft shale of the Skiddaw Slates flattening down into the coastal plain.

The Forestry Commission car park at Bowness Knott is the place to aim for. The road forking from the Loweswater road takes you straight there; from Ennerdale Bridge the signposting is poor - just ignore the first two turnings to the lake and keep going as far as you can. At Bowness Knott there's a map of waymarked forest walks. The most ambitious, Nine Becks, is nearly 10 miles long and climbs to 1,150 feet. Smithy Beck, about an hour and not rising above 215 feet, sounds like the better option.

Ennerdale Water is a reservoir so no boating is allowed. A Forestry Commission leaflet with maps and details of the waymarked trails around the lake is available for 50p from Tourist Information Centres

✪ SKIDDAW

This is the easiest to climb of the 'big four' Lake District peaks that exceed 3,000 feet. If you climb just one major fell, make it this one. When the poet Coleridge lived in Keswick he was forever popping up Skiddaw, but it shouldn't be undertaken lightly. It is a six-mile hike there and back and will take you a good 4-5 hours. The starting place for the simplest ascent is off the A591, just north of the roundabout with the A66. Turn first right, go through Ormathwaite, and take the right turn beyond the driveway to Underscar Manor. There's a car park at the end of this road and the well-trodden route to Skiddaw is signposted 'Skiddaw. Bassenthwaite, Mosedale'. For the first mile or so the path follows the ravine of Whit Beck, flattens out, then climbs more steeply past a series of cairns to the summit. There's a viewing indicator here, and if the visibility is good you should see the Isle of Man to the west, the Pennines to the east and the softened, map-like contours of the Lake District's other peaks.

> Do not miss the easy ascent of **Latrigg**. From the car park take the bridleway south (the opposite direction from Skiddaw). The views from the summit take in the whole of Derwentwater and the deep green Borrowdale valley.

☆ WHINLATTER PASS

This most innocuous of the Lake District's mountain passes starts at Braithwaite to the north-west of Keswick and runs between the Lorton Fells and Grisedale Pike, with excellent views back to Bassenthwaite Lake. On the other side the road continues through the Vale of Lorton and on to Cockermouth.

Much of Whinlatter Pass is Forestry Commission plantations and its highlight is the **Visitor Centre**, recently revamped and aimed very much at children. In the centre itself there's a permanent exhibition on the history, geology and wildlife of Whinlatter. The audio-visual introduction, with commentary in cod-Cumbrian that is virtually incomprehensible, gets the exhibition off to a bad start, but the 'interactive' models and computerised exhibits are well done. In one computer game you take on the role of the forest manager and learn the environmental consequences of elementary decisions - such as whether to clear away dead trees (you can plant new trees in their place) or leave them be, which is good news for the barn owl and yellow wagtail.

Outside the centre there's a human-sized re-creation of a badger sett, and a plethora of forest and mountain bike trails, orienteering courses and ascents to viewpoints such as Grisedale Pike, Lord's Seat and Barf. The routes are marked on the information leaflet available in the centre.

Whinlatter Pass looking east with Skiddaw in the background

The café there, called **The Little Tearoom in the Big Woods**, does take-away food for picnics but the brand new timber building is a congenial place in itself even if the mountain forest theme is a bit over-done: there are photographs of Douglas firs being felled to make the roof beams, notices telling you that the floor is made of oak, the chairs of elm, and the tables of oak, elm, beech and cherry, and the menu features Woodcutter's Soup (vegetable), Lumberjack's Special (soup and a sandwich) and Treetop Toasties. It almost makes you yearn for plastic.

The Whinlatter Pass Visitor Centre is on the B5292 near the top of the pass.
Tel: 07687 78469
Opening times: daily 10am-5.30pm; closed Christmas & Jan. (Times are subject to alteration so it is worth checking first.) The Little Tearoom in the Big Woods is open 10am-7pm Whitsun-end Aug; 10am-5pm rest of the year. The forest trails are always accessible
Admission: free but car parking £1. The information leaflet detailing all the trails is well worth the 80p; there are quiz cards for short children's trails

☆ WYTHOP MILL

This is a former sawmill tucked off a narrow road in a tiny hamlet. There's not a lot going on here but it is worth a visit if only to get you off the A66 Keswick to Cockermouth road and in to some decent scenery that is little visited. The early Victorian waterwheel is a wonderful contraption, known as a 'hybrid' because it is part cast iron (rims and axle) and part wood (linings and buckets). There is something deeply satisfying about watching elderly, unwieldy machinery like this working as well as the day it was installed.

 It is difficult to get as worked up about the static bygones that make up the rest of the exhibition: carding machine, gin traps, butter churns and the like. Still, the coffee shop and licensed restaurant in a converted store room next door do decent snacks and light lunches.

From Wythop Mill to Cockermouth there are two preferable alternatives to the dual carriageway A66. Either cross the A66 and use the old road, wide but now deserted, or continue past the mill, turn right and use the back roads.

Wythop Mill is half a mile south off the A66 four miles from Cockermouth.
Tel: 07687 76394
Opening times: Apr-Oct Tues-Sun 10.30am-5.30pm; winter weekends only; closed Jan & Feb. Restaurant open Apr-Oct Fri & Sat 7-9pm
Admission: adult £1.50; child 70p

WHERE TO STAY

Bassenthwaite Lake
🛥 𝍢 ⛵ 🚲 ££-£££
Bassenthwaite Lakeside Lodges,
Scarness Bay Park, Bassenthwaite Lake, nr Keswick CA12 4QZ
Tel: 07687 76641
Open all year
These wooden cabins make an excellent self-catering option. Not only do they occupy the best lakeside spot on the whole of Bassenthwaite Lake, but all but the basic ones are furnished and equipped to a rare standard, with TV and video, microwave, hair-dryer, and verandah with barbecue. The smartest ones, right on the shore of the lake, even have whirlpool baths - a far cry from the standard tin mobile homes - and the parkland setting teems with rabbits and red squirrels. There's a heated indoor swimming pool, free boating, windsurfing and fishing, mountain bike hire and a video lending library, and the staff are a delight - friendly, enthusiastic and unfailingly helpful. This is not so much caravanning as designer Davy Crockett.

Bassenthwaite Lake
🏠 🕴 ✉ £££

Pheasant Inn, *Bassenthwaite Lake,*
nr Cockermouth, Cumbria CA13 9YE
Tel: 07687 76234
Open all year

Quaintly rustic from the outside,
crisp and elegant inside, the Pheasant
has been putting people up in style
for many years now. There are 17
rooms in the main building and three
in the adjacent bungalow, all done
with refreshing simplicity in light
plain colours and all guaranteeing a
peaceful stay with no TV or telephone. Sizes vary considerably and
the most appealing rooms overlook
the garden and fellside at the back.
Dinner in the candlelit restaurant is a
pretty smart affair and might include
celery and Stilton soup followed by
smoked haddock, hot asparagus
mousse and lime bavarois with
caramel and apricot sauce. There are
three sitting rooms with lots of
antiques and floral fabrics, and a
wonderful bar with walls stained a
deep tobacco brown by generations
of pipe smoke over pre-war wallpaper (the pattern is still just visible)
and sealed in with high-gloss lac-
quer. The effect is even better after a
few pints of real Bass or Theakston's.
Last orders: lunch 1.30pm; dinner
8.30pm.

Cockermouth
🏠 ✕ 🕴 🐾 🚬 £££

Trout Hotel, *Crown Street,*
Cockermouth, Cumbria CA13 0EJ
Tel: 0900 823591
Open all year

The Trout is owned by Mr Mills of
local newsagent fame, which ensures
you get a free morning paper at
Cockermouth's most famous hotel,
next door to Wordsworth House.

Bing Crosby stayed here on a fishing
trip - a picture by the front porch
shows a slightly gormless-looking
Bing holding up a whopper for the
camera. He presumably went for the
olde worlde charm of this long, low
typical Lakeland residence dating
from the late 17th century. Since his
time the interior has been done out
disappointingly downstairs - the
pink velveteen in the bar is particularly unfortunate - but the rooms are
simple and comfortable, if a little
small. Ask for one at the back overlooking the award-winning gardens
and the River Derwent. The four-
course silver service dinners in the
restaurant are reasonably priced and
have an excellent reputation; we
recommend you stick with trout or
salmon, the speciality of the house.
Throughout the year the Trout offers
a number of themed weekend
breaks, such as salmon fishing
courses for beginners. Last orders for
dinner: 9.30pm.

Loweswater
🗯 🕴12 🐄 ✉ £

Brook Farm, *Thackthwaite,*
Loweswater, Cockermouth,
Cumbria CA13 0RP
Tel: 0900 85606
Open May-end Oct

'We've only come 10 times so we're
not sure about it yet,' said one regular couple as they tucked into Mrs
Ann Hayton's delicious shepherd's
pie in the cosy dining cum sitting
room of this old working farmhouse.
At least they have no trouble finding
it - from Cockermouth take the
B5289, take a right at Low Lorton for
Thackthwaite, and Brook Farm is just
before the phone box in the village
itself. The two rooms - one twin, one
double - are basic but perfectly com-

fortable, with excellent views across the lower end of the Vale of Lorton to Grasmoor, Whiteside and Dodd. Loweswater, Crummock Water and Buttermere are just a few minutes by car. There's an option of b & b only, or evening meal as well, both very good value.

Whinlatter Pass
🏠 🚶 🐴 🍴 ££

Cottage in the Wood, *Whinlatter Pass, nr Keswick, Cumbria CA12 5TW*
Tel: 07687 78409
Open Mar-Nov
This former coaching house is on the descent of Whinlatter Pass towards Bassenthwaite, with views of Comb Beck and the wooded valley from the back rooms. It's a delightful spot,

and owners Sandra and Barrie Littlefair have created a special atmosphere which makes you feel more like a house guest than a paying customer. There are just seven rooms - three overlooking the valley and two with four-posters - and all with tasteful, understated decoration of the Laura Ashley type. The five-course set dinners served promptly at 7pm are simple but first-class: pork with orange and cranberry sauce, Scottish salmon, or chicken with sherry sauce for the main course perhaps, followed by tiramisu or sticky toffee pudding. Under-fives must have early tea and under-twelves sharing parents' room are half-price.

WHERE TO EAT

Buttermere
🏠 ✕ 🍴 ££

Bridge Hotel, *Buttermere*
Tel: 07687 70252
Whether you eat in the walkers' bar or go for the five-course dinner in the softly-lit restaurant, the Bridge offers superb local food, and heaps of it. Licensees Peter and Janet McGuire own Lanthwaite Green Farm three miles away, where the beef and lamb are reared. Lakeland specialities include Cumbrian tatie ash - thick lamb and beef stew topped with cold beetroot - beef and beer pie made with Theakston's Old Peculier, and Cumbrian hotpot - lamb, black pudding and potatoes. The restaurant menu also has vegetarian options such as mild bean curry and imaginative salads. The wine list, with a choice of 50 wines, is particularly good. To round it all off, go for the

Old Peculier chocolate fudge cake. The bar serves food all day; restaurant last orders for dinner: 8.30pm.

Cockermouth
🏠 ✕ 🍴 ££

Pickwick Restaurant, *Allerdale Court Hotel, Market Square, Cockermouth*
Tel: 0900 823654
Open all year
A friendly and unfussy restaurant in the centre of Cockermouth using fresh vegetables and home-reared beef from owner Bob Slack's farm. The Dickensian theme is evident in the menu - though chicken Micawber and veal à la Bumble are not perhaps the most felicitous character choices - but the meat dishes such as leg of lakeland lamb are top quality, and to emphasise the freshness the steak diane is cooked at the table. Last orders for dinner 9.30pm.

Cockermouth
✕ 🖃 ££

Quince and Medlar, *13 Castlegate,*
Cockermouth
Tel: 0900 823579
Closed Feb 14-Mar 6 & Mon
On the hill just below the castle, this
award-winning vegetarian restaurant
is light years from the usual stripped
pine and quiche ambience of so
many veggie places. Classical music
plays softly in the background, the
tables are candlelit, and the food is
served with such attention to visual
impact that even avowed meat-eaters
will find it a memorable experience.
The starters - such as avocado profi-
teroles (choux puffs filled with cream
avocado) and fresh fruit medley (seg-
ments of orange, pink grapefruit and
melon styled into a radiant sun) are
perhaps slightly more imaginative
than the main courses. But if dishes
like leek, butterbean and mushroom
casserole or parsnip and cashew nuts
sound more like standard veggie
fare, the sauces of red wine or cider

and herbs redeem them. Even the
elderflower wine tasted good. Last
orders for dinner: 9pm.

Loweswater
🏠 ✕ 🖃 ££

Kirkstile Inn, *Loweswater,*
Cockermouth
Tel: 0900 85219
Open all year
A 16th-century inn next to
Loweswater church and in the shadow of Mellbreak, the Kirkstile offers
a bar menu and four-course dinner in
the restaurant. A typical choice for
the restaurant might be mackerel or
hot grapefruit with brown sugar and
cinnamon, followed by soup or sorbet, and lamb chops as main course.
Despite the views of Mellbreak from
the restaurant, the bar edges it in
terms of atmosphere - low beamed
ceilings, open fire and simple but
hearty fare including children's dishes. Last orders: bar - lunch 2.30pm,
dinner 9pm; restaurant - 8pm.

WASTWATER

The deepest lake, the highest peak, the steepest road, the first nuclear power station...this is a landscape of superlatives. Of contrasts too - from the picturesque valleys of Eskdale and Duddon, to the fells of Wasdale Head and the lonely moors of Corney and Birker Fells. Welcome to England's most rugged and moody corner.

The gateway to it from the east is over the Roman passes of Wrynose and Hardknott - surely one of the most exhilarating drives in Europe. From the other side a good move might be to motor on to Ravenglass on the coast and pick up the Ravenglass & Eskdale narrow gauge railway (nicknamed 'Ratty') which will bring you back and drop you in the heart of Eskdale. Eskdale Mill at Boot, the lovely falls known as Stanley Ghyll Force and the bar food at the George IV Inn are all within striking distance of the Ratty.

But you will need the car to experience the sobering and awesome grandeur of Wastwater, the views of the sea from Corney Fell, the painfully lonely Devoke Water, and the meandering Alpine pocket of the Duddon Valley. And if the weather is unkind there are a couple of thought-provoking places further afield, products of very different ages and ways of thinking: Furness Abbey on the Furness Peninsula, and Sellafield nuclear power station. Finally, for yet more insight on the human condition, don't pass up the chance to stare into the eyes of the owls at Muncaster Castle.

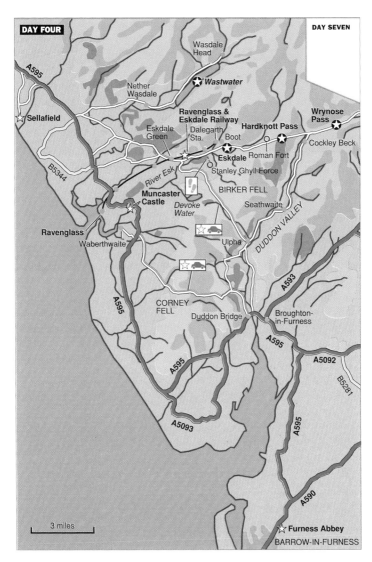

Wasdale
Head

Wastwater

Nether
Wasdale

A595

Sellafield

Ravenglass &
Eskdale Railway

Wrynose
Pass

Eskdale
Green

Dalegarth
Sta.

Hardknott Pass

Boot

Cockley Beck

B5344

Eskdale

Roman Fort

River Esk

Stanley Ghyll Force

Muncaster
Castle

Devoke
Water

BIRKER FELL

Seathwaite

Ravenglass

Waberthwaite

Ulpha

DUDDON VALLEY

A5
93

A595

CORNEY
FELL

Duddon Bridge

Broughton-
in-Furness

A595

A5092

B5281

A5093

A595

A590

3 miles

Furness Abbey

BARROW-IN-FURNESS

CORNEY FELL DRIVE

This drive starts at Waberthwaite, south of Ravenglass on the
A595, but before setting off it is worth seeking out a shop called
Woodall's. This is the home of a Rolls-Royce among bangers
called the Waberthwaite Cumberland sausage, served in all the

best eateries in the Lakes and regularly consumed by the Queen - the nondescript terrace shop proudly bears the royal coat of arms. The shop has been here since 1828 and is now in the seventh generation of the Woodall family. Their secret is to stick to traditional dry-curing methods, using salt and saltpetre, and age-old recipes - the sausages are 100 per cent meat, with no rusk or water. Other delicacies include Cumbria air-dried ham, matured for 12 months and rather like Parma, and Mature Royal ham, cured in a pickle of old ale and molasses. The shop is as venerable as the recipes - the furniture and counters that were ripped out 40 years ago have recently been restored and re-instated. 'It's what you call going backwards,' said Richard Woodall.

Woodall's is at Lane End, Waberthwaite, a sharp right-hand turn off the A595
Opening times: 8.30am-5.30pm Mon-Fri (closed 12.15-1.15pm for lunch); Sat 8.30am-noon

Return north along the A595 and take a sharp right-hand turn for Corney Fell. The road runs across the top of the fell for nearly ten miles to Duddon Bridge (ignore turnings to left and right). This is an old-fashioned sort of drive for which you really need a travelling rug across the knees to complete the effect. The wind howls across the lonely uninhabited landscape, the views west to the Irish Sea and east to the Duddon valley are spectacular, but the cocoon of the car is definitely the best place to be.

Corney Fell looking towards the Duddon Estuary

Duddon Bridge Iron Furnace

On the descent to Duddon Bridge is one of the finest intact relics of traditional Lakeland industry. The **Duddon Bridge Iron Furnace** was built in 1736 as a blast furnace, using charcoal fuel from the vast coppice woodlands roundabout, and closed in 1867. It seems astonishing that it was in operation so long ago - a truly dark satanic mill in an idyllic spot carpeted by bluebells in April, and predating the Industrial Revolution by 100 years or more. The furnace itself is a fascinating construction: a brick beehive 28 feet high and 12 feet in diameter, tapering to 3 feet at the top. The site is administered by the National Park Authority which is anxious that it shouldn't become over-run with sightseers. The plan is to erect an 'interpretive panel' on the bridleway next to it, with simple cast iron labels on the main buildings, but not to promote it in any way, so please respect the integrity of the place. As the National Park's conservation officer, Andrew Lowe, says: 'The aim is to provide only basic information so that the solitary walker may still come across these buildings unexpectedly - like a temple in a forest.'

Duddon Bridge Iron Furnace is just off the Corney Fell Road on the opposite side from the River Duddon, before the T junction with the A595. The only indication is a bridleway sign

☆ DUDDON VALLEY & BIRKER FELL DRIVE

A low-level alternative to the gruelling Hardknott Pass, this V-shaped detour will take you from Wrynose Bottom to Eskdale. Though avoiding the 1 in 3 gradient of Hardknott may be recommendation enough for some, the drive is a delight in its own right. From Cockley Beck (before the road from Wrynose rises towards Hardknott) take the Seathwaite and Ulpha road which follows the course of the **Duddon Valley.** The River Duddon rises on the summit of Wrynose, and marks the old boundary between Lancashire, to the east, and Cumberland (now it's all Cumbria). At Dunnerdale Forest car park there are picnic benches alongside the Duddon and a signboard with waymarked paths to Harter Fell, Hardknott and the forest itself, all starting at Birks Bridge 200 yards to the south. Beyond Birks Bridge the valley becomes very picturesque, not to say Alpine, the wooded ravine plunging to the fast flowing river on the western side while the road rises to the east.

Through Seathwaite the road reaches Ulpha. Ignore, for the moment, the turn to the right signposted to Eskdale Green and continue on to the intimate and ancient **Church of St John, Ulpha**. Standing on the banks of the River Duddon on a bend in the road before the bridge, it is simply whitewashed inside, with old roof timbers and amateurish illustrated inscriptions from the 18th century. (Our forebears seem so good at drawing and writing on the whole that it's refreshing to find some who evidently weren't.) Wordsworth got here before us and made sure we would know about it by writing a sonnet, *Kirk of Ulpha*, part of the Duddon Valley series.

The river continues on to its outlet on Duddon Sands some six miles to the south, while this detour takes you back to the turn for Eskdale Green. As the road climbs the steep hill out of Ulpha it leaves behind the verdant valley bottom and reaches a plateau of bleak moorland, **Birker Fell**, where the wind always blows, and there's always rain in the air. The contrast is an example of how suddenly and utterly the landscape changes with altitude. With occasional undulations the road runs flat for five miles or so before descending to Eskdale Green and rejoining the more direct westerly route over Hardknott.

The scenery up here has its own forbidding beauty, nowhere more so than round **Devoke Water**. This mountain tarn is rarely visited, probably because there is no signpost to it and it is not visible from the road. Park by the signpost pointing to Stanley Ghyll that says 'Not suitable for motors' and follow the track on the opposite (west) side of the road. Devoke Water hoves into view after half-a-mile's level walking. John Ruskin talked of his 'intense joy, mingled with awe' on first setting eyes on this sanctuary of water - a pronouncement that surely postdates the mislaying of his marbles, for nowhere could be less joyful than Devoke Water. Its shores are flat, boggy, treeless, and lashed by rain driven straight off the Atlantic. The sole human element is a stone-built boathouse on the south side, pitifully small beneath the dark eminence of The Seat, and all the more forlorn for being obviously derelict. It's only a couple of miles or so round the tarn (clockwise is best) but it takes a good two hours because the paths are so boggy you have constantly to retrace your steps to find higher, drier ground. Crossing its outlet, Linbeck Gill, at the western end can be tricky - the gill is narrow but fast flowing and quite deep - but you should be able to pick your way across on the rocks.

● ESKDALE

This long green corridor running to the sea is the reward for surviving Hardknott Pass, its main access road from the east. The valley head is under the fells that cradle Hardknott, and its main attractions lie between here and the village of Eskdale Green as the landscape shades from wild and craggy fells to meadows and mixed woodland.

Boot, which is a dead-end off the valley road, was an industrial centre when iron ore was mined in the fellsides above and brought down to the village by perpendicular railway in the last century. It is also home to **Eskdale Cornmill**, which worked from the 16th century until its closure in the 1920s. Now the mill is a museum owned by the County Council, reached by a little packhorse bridge at the north end of the village. Unusually, it has two wheels, side by side. The museum consists of a moderately interesting exhibition on the social and industrial past of the mill and the valley, but the location is what really makes it worthwhile. There's a wooded picnic area at the back by the weir, waterfalls, and a deep pool with a natural diving board formed by cliffs some 30 feet above.

Eskdale Cornmill, Boot. Tel: 09467 23335
Opening times: Easter-late Sept 11am-5 pm (often until 8pm in summer); closed Mon
Admission: adult £1; child 5-16 50p

Opposite the Burnmoor Inn, the **Fold End Gallery** in Boot is a cut above the usual arts and crafts places. The tiny stone building was a stable and the entrance is reached by an outside staircase. Whatever your tastes - and the paintings, ceramics, sculpture and jewellery cannot be to everyone's - at least the work here is executed with integrity and skill and there is little that's offensively cute or sentimental. Much of it is by local artists on local themes, but regular exhibitors come from far and wide. Open 10am-5.30pm daily except Monday.

DALEGARTH FALLS WALK

One of the valley's outstanding natural features is the waterfall known variously as Dalegarth Falls or Stanley Ghyll Force. Past Dalegarth Station (now the terminus for the Ravenglass & Eskdale Railway - see separate entry) take the left turn opposite the Eskdale Centre. There's a car park just beyond where the road crosses the River Esk. Continue on foot, bearing left past the entrance to a house, and keep going till you reach a wood where there's a signpost for the falls. The path follows the course of the stream, becoming steeper and edged with mossy boulders, and rhododendrons crowd in from the steep sides of the ravine. The wooden bridges criss-crossing the stream lend the walk an air of childhood adventure. The final bridge, high up towards the falls, has been out of action since bad storms in 1987 brought trees crashing down into the ravine. Instead cross by the lower bridge (ducking under a fallen tree on the other side) and loop back and round. The path leads to a lip of rocks jutting above the precipice at the angle of a sunbed and veined with tree roots, with the falls crashing beyond a curtain of rhododendrons. This is exhilarating but dangerous and small children and dogs should be kept well back. If you can master the vertigo, stand up and look north into the valley - the white building looking so spick and span is the Brook House Hotel at Boot. Return the same way - the walk is less than two miles and should take you under an hour.

The roads of Eskdale have been trodden for many thousands of years - by Neolithic Man, Romans and Vikings - and the site of the **King George IV Inn** has been a watering hole for almost as long. Well placed at the T-junction of the Hardknott road and the road through Eskdale Green to the port of Ravenglass, the 18th-century building has a Roman well in the cellar alongside the barrels of Bass, Boddington's and Theakston's. There's a warren of bars on different levels, stone-flagged in the oldest part, an open log fire, and a fearsome-looking plough on one wall. The food is local and good, and there's lots of it: Waberthwaite Cumberland sausage and egg, home-baked Cumberland ham, home-cured gammon with free-range eggs, superior sandwiches, and tempting puddings like Marsala ice cream with brandy snaps. There is also a children's menu and half portions of most main courses are available. Food is served daily noon-2pm and 7-9pm.

☆ FURNESS ABBEY

This mediaeval monastery is quite a drive from the Wastwater area, but worth it if you like ecclesiastical ruins and the history that goes with them. The interesting thing about Furness is that it was the second-richest Cistercian monastery in England (after Fountains in Yorkshire) before Henry VIII got his hands on it. In its heyday the abbey owned and farmed vast tracts of the Lake District, including Eskdale and Borrowdale. Now its domain is

Mediaeval Furness Abbey

confined to the beautiful and atmospheric valley, the Vale of the Deadly Nightshade, in which its rust-red ruins stand. Much of it is well preserved, especially the church, and the Walkman audio-tour leads you carefully through them, pausing by such high-lights as the five Norman arches on the south side of the clois-ters. Furness was quite a tourist attraction in Victorian times - a railway was constructed specially to ferry in the hordes - but is rather neglected now. Wordsworth wrote a poem about it, of course, and it happens to be the resting place of King Reginald of the Isle of Man - not a lot of people know that.

Furness Abbey is a left turn off the A590 on the outskirts of Barrow. Tel: 0229 823420
Opening times: Apr 1-end Sept daily 10am-6pm; in winter 10am-4pm, closed Mon
Admission: adult £1.60; child 5-16 80p

☆ MUNCASTER CASTLE

From the castle terrace the views of Eskdale, with the river snaking and widening towards the sea, may be magnificent, but to the barn-owl they spell disaster: the dense woodlands and ungrazed grasslands in which the barn owl needs to live and hunt are long gone, and this beautiful bird is now facing extinc-tion. This point is made forcefully by Tony Warburton, director of the **Owl Centre** based at Muncaster Castle. The centre styles itself a 'Noah's Ark' for owls and other breeds and is the head-quarters of the British Owl Breeding and Release Scheme (BOBARS). The indigenous owls kept here are studied, bred, and where appropriate released into the wild. Foreign species have been rescued from threatened habitats such as the Gulf or the South American rainforests - their lot may be to remain cooped in cages, but the alternative was no life at all. These magnificent and dignified creatures, some sitting like potentates, others like heraldic devices, seem to see right to the core of man's ecological folly with their unblinking eyes.

Weather permitting, there is a 'Meet the Birds' flying display on the castle lawns at 2.30pm every day, featuring a kestrel, a buz-zard, a barn owl and sometimes a tawny owl. Membership of BOBARS costs £7.50 a year. It is also possible to 'adopt an owl', which costs from £25 a year. Tony Warburton's Owl Centre - indeed, the owls themselves - need all the help and support they can get.

Muncaster Castle itself, some of it dating from the 13th century, is owned by a delightful triple-barrelled family called the Gordon-Duff-Penningtons. They also still live here - the border collie curled on the sofa in the galleried octagonal library is real, not stuffed, and the same may be said for the lady who often sits quietly in the corner of the leather-lined dining room, for it is none other than Mrs G-D-P. The Walkman audio-tour is worth sticking with for the occcasional and candid interjections by Mr G-D-P, who will tell you how when it gets 'beastly cold' he and the wife huddle round the fire draped in sleeping bags to keep warm. Surrounding the castle are nearly 80 acres of gardens and woodlands with rhododendrons - at their best in May - , a garden centre, an adventure playground, a heronry, and a Nature Trail.

Muncaster Castle and Owl Centre is off the A595 a mile east of Ravenglass.
Tel: Castle - 0229 717614; Owl Centre - 0229 717393
Opening times: castle - Mar 27-Nov 7 Tues-Sun 1-4pm; gardens and Owl Centre daily all year 11am-5pm
Admission: for castle, gardens and Owl Centre - adult £4.50; child £2.50; family ticket £12; gardens and Owl Centre only - adult £2.80; child £1.50; family ticket £7.50

RAVENGLASS & ESKDALE RAILWAY

Known locally as 'Ratty' (probably after a Mr Ratcliffe who built it to serve the iron ore mines in Eskdale) this narrow-gauge railway, using both steam and diesel engines, runs from the port of Ravenglass to Dalegarth in the heart of the valley. The seven-mile journey takes 40 minutes so this is not exactly the Flying Scotsman - and describing it as 'the most beautiful train journey in England' is a bit overstated. But it's a pleasant if unspectacular ride through gentle countryside, and the only irritation is likely to be the tribes of little monsters of the peashooter-and-catapult tendency, off-loaded by frazzled parents who pick them up at the other end.

The journey is best done eastwards, from Ravenglass, so the fells and scenery of central Lakeland unfold gradually as you progress. Ravenglass station is a nice old place, tranquil and pre-Beeching, with a rather comical museum telling the story of the Ratty line. There's an exhibit of the mining operation at Boot, complete with bewhiskered Action Men dressed up as iron-ore miners, and a poster from 1925 exhorting day-trippers to 'Visit the highest mountain [Sca Fell], the deepest lake [Wastwater] and almost the smallest church [Wasdale Head] in England'.

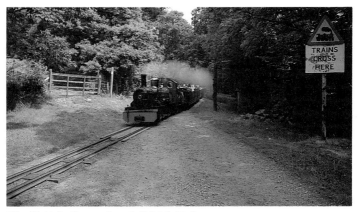

The 'Ratty' - Ravenglass & Eskdale Railway

To reinforce the Toy Town feel of the Ratty, first stop is **Muncaster Mill**, 'one of the oldest working businesses in the UK', according to jovial miller Robert Park. Fed by a race from the adjacent River Mite, it started as an oatmill in 1455 (the present building dates from about 1700), ceased to function in 1961 and was restored to working order by the Eskdale Trust in 1978. Now the mill produces its own bran, semolina, wholemeal, unbleached white flour and coarse oatmeal, all of which are on sale. Robert Park will give you a tour of the 19th-century millstones and bemusing system of cogged gears, and the thirsty waterwheel that requires two million gallons of water a day to drive them. Afterwards it's a pleasant spot to linger before boarding the next Ratty - there are picnic tables, a pond fished by a heron, and walks along the bank of the River Mite.

The Ravenglass & Eskdale Railway Co Ltd, Ravenglass. Tel: 0229 717171
Running times: daily Apr 3-Oct 31 - first steam-hauled train from Ravenglass
10.25am (except Sun), last steam-hauled train 4.15pm; Nov-Mar, mostly weekends
only. Timetables are complicated so you are advised to telephone to check
Prices: adult £5.20 return; child £2.60; Eskdale Explorer ticket for a family of 4 £13
Muncaster Mill is on the A595 one mile north-east of Ravenglass. Tel: 0229 717232
Opening times: Apr, May, Sept, Oct, 11am-5pm daily except Sat; June, Jul &Aug
10am-6pm daily except Sat; other times by appointment
Admission: adult £1.20; child 60p

SELLAFIELD

There is nothing like a change of scenery. And it's remarkable how utterly the scenery changes in the handful of miles from the edge of the National Park to the unlovely Cumbrian coast dominated by the world's first nuclear power station. It was Calder Hall back in 1952. Now it is Sellafield (out of Windscale), which tells us something of how this industrial metropolis has attempted to redefine itself as it has grown and the controversy surrounding it has intensified. The really suspicious thing about the Visitors' Centre is not that BNFL feels the need to have one, but that it is entirely free. The real risk of exposure is not to radiation, but to defensive propaganda, on which there has evidently been no expense spared.

The centre, which could double as a film set for *Dr Who*, consists of a series of futuristic chambers and walkways with working models, multi-screen video presentations, computer games and quizzes - most of it geared to reassuring you that the risks inherent in the nuclear game are laughably minimal. Afterwards there's a coach tour of the plant itself, cloaked in rather bogus security precautions. Cameras are not allowed - they will be collected on board the coach by the guide - and identity forms have to be completed and handed in at a checkpoint charlie before entering the plant. You are not allowed to get off the coach during the 35-minute tour. Instead the guide explains the various buildings and their functions, ranging from the seriously apocalyptic - the military pile closed down after a fire in 1957 - to the mundane (wages office, laundry).

The Sellafield Visitors' Centre is a turn off the A595 at Calder Bridge.
Tel: 09467 27027
Opening times: daily all year; Nov-Mar 10am-4pm, Apr-Oct 10am-6pm
Admission: free

WASTWATER

The first-time visitor is liable to reach for some such adjective as 'symphonic' to do justice to the grandeur of Wastwater and its backcloth of fells (they even reduced Wordsworth to silence). This is the deepest lake in England (some 250 feet) and is ringed at its head by three monstrous fells, Great Gable, Scafell and

Scafell Pike (England's highest peak at 3,206 feet). There are two approaches - from Santon Bridge, which meets the lake head on, or from Gosforth which brings you on to the north-west shore opposite the famous fan-shaped screes falling all but sheer for 1,700 feet. The drive along the shore is surprisingly domesticated, fringed with gorse and hawthorn bushes, Scots pines and broad-leaved trees, and with plenty of parking and picnic places. The road leads to Wasdale Head, honorary headquarters of British rockclimbing, where there's the wonderful Wasdale Head Inn (see Where to Eat). Across a field to the east of the inn is the tiny church (40 feet long and 17 feet wide), enclosed and hidden by a ring of yew trees, and the resting place of climbers killed on the fells.

Wastwater, England's deepest lake

This is hairy-chested walking country, with little in the way of gentle rambles. The best bet for a walk is to go back towards the other end of the lake and park at the main viewpoint opposite the screes, where the road joins from Gosforth. From here walk south along the shore in front of the Youth Hostel (Wasdale Hall) and round a grassy promontory. The views back towards the head of the lake are - well, symphonic.

Canoes and rowing boats only are allowed on Wastwater. Permits are available from the campsite at the head of the lake. Contact campsite warden 9-10am Easter-Oct; tel: 09467 26220

WRYNOSE AND HARDKNOTT PASSES

You can't claim to have 'done' the Lake District without undergoing the ordeal by gradient otherwise known as Wrynose and Hardknott. These two passes were forged by the Romans as an important trade route between Ambleside and the port of Ravenglass. Now they are the most direct way of reaching the western lakes and the west coast from the centre of the Lake District - so there's no excuse unless your car has a dodgy transmission or brakes.

Wrynose Pass rises in the east at the meeting point of Little and Great Langdale, near Fell Foot farm. It starts easily enough, but beyond Wrynose Bridge, where there's just about room enough to stop and turn round if you have second thoughts, the gradient becomes severe (first gear all the way) and there are some pretty hairy drops to the side. On the top is the Three Shires Stone, marking the meeting place of the boundaries of Cumberland, Westmoreland and Lancashire (before the local government shake-up of 1974). There's also a parking place, and it's worth getting out and walking back to the ridge which has views east into Little Langdale and the tarn there.

Hardknott Fort and Hardknott Pass

The flat, featureless hanging valley on the other side called Wrynose Bottom is the lull before the storm of **Hardknott Pass**. If you wish to bale out, do so at Cockley Beck by taking the Ulpha road (see Duddon Valley Drive). Hardknott has switchbacks with gradients of 1 in 3 and the climb is longer than Wrynose, but the reward is a stunning view of the Eskdale Valley coiling like a fat green serpent towards the sea. Wrynose and Hardknott are best avoided in high season, when problems can be caused by fellow drivers stalling in front of you and an insufficient number of passing places for the volume of traffic. In any case the best way to experience these highways in the sky is on your own, at dawn or dusk.

On the western descent of Hardknott look out for the Roman **Hardknott Fort**, built on a grassy shelf of fellside to the north of the road to guard the mountain pass. The remains are not up to much, but the location is exhilarating. Park on the right-hand side of the road after the first steep descent from the summit. Access to the fort, known as *Mediobogdum*, is about 100 yards further down the road. Beyond the bathhouse is the fort itself, built in a square about the size of a football pitch with entry gates on the north-west and south-east sides. The gate on the far side was presumably for the sake of symmetry only as it opens onto a precipice from which there are great views across to the Scafell mountains. While you are here, spare a thought for the Roman squaddie, billeted far from home in this northern fastness and no doubt dreaming of wine and concubines.

WHERE TO STAY

In general the area is poorly served for accommodation. What there is tends to fill up with BNFL employees working at Sellafield so it is advisable to book well in advance.

Duddon Valley
⌂ � ⛷ ✕ £

Dower House, *High Duddon, Broughton-in-Furness, Cumbria*
Tel: 0229 716279
Open all year
This Victorian mansion is in a lovely spot towards the base of the Duddon Valley. It stands in six acres of woodlands across the road from the river, and has a beck diverted to flow through the garden. There's nothing grand about the Dower House but the set-up is unusual - the rooms are divided into apartments consisting of two bedrooms, bathroom, sitting

room and kitchen, which makes ideal accommodation for a family or two couples sharing. Otherwise the rooms can be let individually on a b & b basis, using a shared bathroom. The owner Mrs Barton mixes and matches according to demand. Apartments as well as bedrooms can be let by the night or by the week, and there's a restaurant for those who prefer not to self-cater. A nice touch is the bar, open from 7pm, where guests help themselves and enter their drinks in a book.

Eskdale

Woolpack Inn, *Boot, Eskdale, Cumbria CA19 1TH*
Tel: 09467 23230
Closed week preceding Christmas
This black and white Lakeland inn is just about the first sign of civilisation following the descent from Hardknott - and a welcome one it is. The Woolpack is a friendly, no-nonsense place facing Harter Fell, with eight simple rooms set around an airy skylit landing. One is a family apartment of two adjoining rooms. All have tea- and coffee-making facilities and hand-basins and half have en suite bathrooms, while the bathtub in the shared bathroom is big enough to re-enact Trafalgar. Downstairs there's the Dalesman Bar with real ales, a residents' lounge with antique grandfather clock, and a restaurant with an open range serving good home-cooked food. Food is also available in the Dalesman Bar - people come from miles around for the Woolpack chips apparently. Oh, and just outside lives a mad goat called Skippy. Restaurant last orders for dinner: 8.30pm.

Nether Wasdale

Low Wood Hall Hotel, *Nether Wasdale, Cumbria CA20 1ET*
Tel: 09467 26289
Closed Christmas Eve - mid-Jan
This secluded hotel on the lower slopes facing across Nether Wasdale was built by a Whitehaven brewer in the mid-19th century. Downstairs it still exudes the atmosphere of a J B Priestley play about northern mill-owners, with original gas chandeliers, marble fireplaces and stained glass. There's a large dining room in the conservatory overlooking the terrace and gardens, a drawing room, and a purpose-built billiard room with pool table and three-quarter size snooker table. The bedrooms are disappointingly characterless in comparison. Last orders for dinner: 8.45pm.

Ravenglass

Muncaster Mill, *Ravenglass, Cumbria CA18 1ST*
Tel: 0229 717232
Open all year
This is handy for the Ratty line apart from being a delightful spot next to the River Mite, and Mr and Mrs Park are a congenial couple who are guaranteed to make you feel part of the family. It comprises just a double and a twin room which share a large bathroom, but the bonus here is the tranquil setting - with walks up the river where you might be lucky enough to see mink, feral cats and deer - and the breakfasts. Bread comes freshly baked that morning from the mill next door, and the sausages are courtesy of the inimitable Mr Woodall of Waberthwaite. No evening meals. No smoking.

Wastwater

🏠 🔥 🐎 🛏 £££

Wasdale Head Inn, *Wasdale Head, Gosforth, Cumbria CA20 1EX*
Tel: 09467 26229
Closed mid-Nov - Dec 26 & mid-Jan - mid-Mar

You have to at least *pretend* to be a serious walker if you stay here, for the Wasdale Head is geared to pampering tired limbs and feeding cavernous stomachs after a day out on Great Gable or the Scafells. The roomy pine-panelled bedrooms are a pleasing combination of the functional and luxurious, all with showers or baths and toilets, lots of storage space for boots and rucksacks, and magnificent views whichever side you're on. There's a drying room with spin dryer for fumigating sodden socks, and a cosy lounge with open fire and a good library overlooking the garden. This leads to Mosedale Beck which has a natural swimming pool. The dark and atmospheric Ritson's Bar, decorated with climbing paraphernalia and old photographs, fills up with walkers and climbers quaffing ale and swapping stories. The Wasdale Head also owns a number of self-catering cottages close by, available on a weekly basis throughout the year.

WHERE TO EAT

Broughton-in-Furness

✗ 🛏 £££

Beswicks Restaurant, *Langholme House, The Square, Broughton-in-Furness*
Tel: 0229 716285
Closed 1st 2 wks May & usually Sun-Tues

Village squares in the Lake District are a rarity for some reason, but Broughton's is a little beauty, shaded by chestnut trees. And on the corner is a classy little joint called Beswicks where the food matches the quiet elegance of the surroundings. The bar cum lounge on the ground floor has marshmallow sofas, soft floral prints and an open-grate fire. Downstairs shades of red predominate in the low-ceilinged cellar restaurant, which has candles and flowers on the tables and manages to be intimate without being cramped. The five-course menu changes every 4-6 weeks and might start with avocado garnished with crab, tomato and onion salad or smoked venison with pâté, followed by soup and home-baked bread, supreme of pigeon sautéed with bacon, onions and tarragon, or halibut steak baked with vermouth, the cheese board (the Stilton is succulent), and puddings such as gâteau ganache, date and ginger pudding or mostly home-made sorbets and ice cream. There's more seating upstairs if it gets busy, but try to eat in the cellar bar. Last orders for dinner 9pm.

Eskdale

🍴 🛏 ££

Bower House Inn, *Eskdale, Holmrook*
Tel: 09467 23244
Open all year

This lovely old coaching inn in the heart of Eskdale is traditionally English without being precious or stuffy about it. It is next to the village cricket field, with lawns framed with fruit trees, an old-fashioned bar with French windows opening onto the lawn, and restaurant that is more like a country house kitchen. Bar and restaurant menus are separate, though left-overs from the restaurant are served in the bar the following night (and probably best avoided for this reason). The bar food is pretty standard fare - open sandwiches, ploughman's, gammon steak, egg and chips - but the restaurant is rather special: try the pork in cider or wild duck and leave room for some bread and butter pudding or Grand Marnier mousse. A conference centre is attached to the inn, which tends to fill up with executives from the Sellafield nuclear plant. Last orders: bar - lunch 2pm; dinner 9.30pm; restaurant - dinner 8.30pm.

Wastwater
⌂ ✕ 🗖 £££
Wasdale Head Inn, *Wasdale Head, Gosforth*
Tel: 09467 26229
Closed mid-Nov - Boxing Day and mid-Jan - mid-Mar
A limited but delicious and healthy menu is available in the restaurant overlooking Great Gable and Sty Head. For starters there might be a choice of salads or smoked Buttermere eel with hot apple sauce, followed by soup or sorbet, roast beef or wild mushroom casserole, pudding and cheese and biscuits. Orders are taken in the panelled residents' bar, which serves good real ale, or there's a very good wine list. The Wasdale Head is also one of the friendliest places encountered in the Lakes. Last orders for dinner 8pm.

CONISTON

Beatrix Potter made this area her own, and bequeathed much of it to us via the National Trust. It is all very pretty, like her books. For once the area's principal town - Hawkshead - is as attractive as the landscape that surrounds it, and if Coniston is a less dramatic lake than many, its very own Steam Yacht, *Gondola*, gives the smoothest ride this side of Venice.

Hawkshead is that rarity in the Lakes, a town of genuine architectural interest. Its winding lanes are free of traffic, leaving you to wander without fear of a wing mirror up the backside, though the human traffic jams can get pretty unbearable. The famous beauty spot of Tarn Hows nearby gets similarly over-run. Though Hawkshead and Coniston are less central than Windermere or Ambleside, they are too accessible to escape the crowds.

Five years before Beatrix Potter and her imaginary menagerie moved into Hill Top at Near Sawrey, John Ruskin died a troubled and lonely man at Brantwood on the shore of Coniston. The house, and the nature trail behind it, are now one of the biggest draws in the area, though what Ruskin would have made of the tourist invasion doesn't bear thinking about. When you tire of all the bookishness, the brasserie there will set you up for the afternoon.

Grizedale Forest Visitors' Centre caters for brains and brawn alike. The walks and mountain bike trails cover huge tracts of forest (the strange objects and creatures you will find there are not hallucinations but sculptures) while the Theatre in the Forest offers more mainstream culture, in the form of classical and jazz evenings.

If you venture farther afield, the market town of Ulverston boasts a gem of a museum devoted to the immortal comedy double act of Laurel and Hardy. Oh, if Ruskin had been alive to see them.

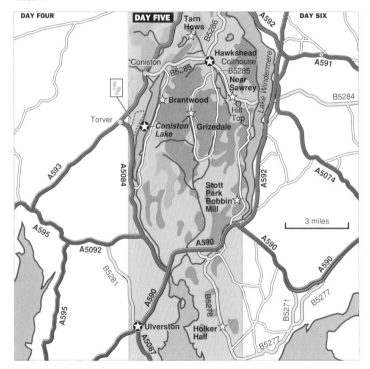

☆ BRANTWOOD

Perched on the north-eastern shore of Coniston, this gleaming white mansion was the home of Victorian polymath John Ruskin from 1872 until his death in 1900. According to Tolstoy he was 'one of those rare men who think with their hearts' but Ruskin was too clever by half. 'I'm almost sick and giddy with the quantity of things in my head,' he said once. In the end he blew a gasket and lived out his days in a wheelchair in the turret on the south-west corner of Brantwood, gazing out across the lake. Standing where that wheelchair once stood, you can feel the brilliant, troubled presence of a man whose range of abilities and interests was astonishing. The video introduction sketches his achievements as artist, poet, critic and social reformer. The walls of the house are filled with his paintings and drawings, from architectural details to dreamy landscapes, but regrettably many of his own collection of books and paintings - including the Turner watercolours that once hung in his bedroom - have been sold off.

The rooms open to the public are the drawing room - containing many of his own pictures, the library - built after Ruskin's death, in 1905, the great man's study, the dining room with its seven beautiful lancet windows, the old dining room containing an introductory exhibition, and Ruskin's bedrooms. Take time to stand in the turret. There's scarcely a better view anywhere in the Lakes. It's important to visit Brantwood in reasonable weather because the Brantwood Nature Trail is a gem. But before doing it, visit the **Ice House**, an egg-shaped chamber 13 feet high hewn from the solid rock of the fellside which served as a primitive refrigerator. (Watch the steps up to it when it is wet as they can be treacherous.) The ice it used was probably local, though other 19th-century ice houses imported ice from Norway or New England. Typically, Ruskin had it built not so much for himself as for the use of the local poor - he was a rare combination of misanthropy and generosity.

The **Nature Trail** covers three miles of the Brantwood estate, as far as the summit of Crag Head, and should take about two hours. It includes broad-leaved woods, remnants of ancient industry such as mediaeval iron-works, charcoal-burning platforms and kilns for baking bricks, and a huge variety of trees, plants and wildlife. The ravine of Beck Leven is a sheltered and damp micro-climate which makes a perfect habitat for exotic toadstools, garlic and wild strawberries. From Crag Head there are good views across the lake to Coniston Old Man and (weather permitting) Helvellyn to the north. On the way down look out for rare insect-munching plants called the sundew and the butterwort, and Ruskin's stone seat next to the waterfall.

Brantwood is on the eastern shore of Lake Coniston. Tel: 05394 41396
Opening times: daily mid-Mar - mid-Nov 11am-5.30 pm
Admission: adult £2.80; child under 7 free

Housed in the old Brantwood stables, the **Jumping Jenny Tearooms and Brasserie** is a delightful place for lunch. Everything here is just so - the stable stalls now form private booths, the decor is a relaxing cornflower blue and cream, there are pre-Raphaelite prints on the walls, flowers on the tables, and opera playing softly in the background. No detail is overlooked - the bread rolls are warmed, the individual butter pats bear sprigs of parsley. The menu ranges from imaginative sandwiches to tagliatelle with meat or vegetable sauce, steak and kidney pudding, and game pie cassoulet, and puddings such as Aunt Grace's Pavlova and fresh fruit tarts. Open April 1 to mid-November 10.30am-6pm; also 7.30-10pm on Wednesday, Friday and Saturday during June, July and August; winter Wednesday-Sunday 11am-4pm. Tel: 05394 41715.

✪ CONISTON LAKE

It's important to remember that the Lake District had a rich industrial identity before the advent of tourism. Coniston village, its lake and valley were a centre for iron smelting, copper mining and slate quarrying as well as farming. And if visitors find this grey slate village rather tatty and disappointing, who are we to dictate that it should conform to a cute touristy blueprint? That said, the village is not a place to waste time in. Its cafés, shops and pubs are dreary - though it has some fine guesthouses - and surprisingly it makes little of its most famous adoptive son, Donald Campbell, who killed himself making a reckless attempt on the world waterspeed record in January 1967.

The **Ruskin Museum** typifies the malaise of the place. From the outside it looks like a public loo, and inside it smells rather like one. The jumble of Ruskin memorabilia is poorly labelled, in faded handwriting or peeling Dymotape, and all sorts of other odds and ends have found their way in with little apparent rhyme or reason. The most interesting items are the preliminary sketches for Ruskin's memorial cross in Coniston churchyard, a pagan-looking sculpture with pre-Raphaelite flourishes.

The Ruskin Museum is up a lane just beyond, and opposite, the Tourist Information Centre
Opening times: week before Easter-end Oct, Sun-Fri 11am-1pm, 2-5pm
Admission: adult £1; child 50p

The best escape route from the village is on the **Steam Yacht Gondola,** which leaves from Coniston Pier and takes just under an hour to circle the lake. *Gondola* is easily the finest of the Lake District's steamers - 'the perfect combination of the Venetian gondola and the English steam yacht' according to the *Illustrated London News* when she was launched in 1859. She remained in service till 1937 when she became a houseboat. After being ravaged by storms in 1963 she was lovingly restored by the National Trust and returned to service in 1980. The ride she gives is elegant, low in the water and extraordinarily smooth while the throb of the engines is barely perceptible. The saloons inside are divided rather like an old pub - padded seats, upholstered ceiling, carpets in the 'lounge', bare boards in the 'public bar' towards the stern. There are also uncovered seats in bows and stern, and these are the best bet unless it's cold or wet, though people tend to move around once she's underway. She has two stopping-off points - Park-a-Moor and Brantwood - and a good tip in high season is to embark at Brantwood. This is the stop before the return to Coniston Pier and ensures you beat the crowds waiting there for the next trip.

Coniston Lake

Hawkshead Parish Church

Coniston Lake is five miles long, half a mile wide at its widest point, and reaches depths of 180 feet. Somewhere down there is Donald Campbell, who favoured Coniston because it was the straightest of the lakes, with just one small island. Campbell's doomed attempt on the world waterspeed record a quarter of a century ago has already achieved a folkloric quality. Though wreckage from *Bluebird* was washed up, Campbell's body was never recovered. Travelling on *Gondola*, it's hard to impute a murderous intent to the waters of Coniston. The views from *Gondola* are slightly disappointing, but the experience of gliding so close to the water is the real treat.

Coniston Pier is a short distance from the village and there's plenty of parking space. Tel 05394 41288 to check on sailings as Gondola does not sail in bad weather
Sailing times: daily Apr 1-Nov 1, starting at 11am except Sat when she starts at 12.05pm. Last sailings: 2.50pm until May 1 and 2nd wk Sept-Nov 1; 4pm in summer
Fares (payable on board): adult £4 for round trip; child £2.40; family ticket for up to 6 £12.50
Coniston Boating Centre next to the pier has a variety of boats for hire. Tel: 05394 41366
Rowing boats are from £2.40 an hour; sailing dinghies from £8.50; cabin motor boats from £10.30; 'Mystic' electric launches from £13
Summitreks (05394 41212) in Yewdale Road, Coniston has canoes for hire for £8.50 for three hours; windsurfers for £14
The lake has a speed limit of 10mph

CONISTON WALK

The best way to see the lake is far from the crowds at Coniston village and Brantwood, along the western shore. Take the A593 from the village and branch left on the A5084 at Torver. Park in the car park opposite a Land Rover garage and pass through a gate on to Torver Back Common. The path passes to the left of a pond and up a hill to the right of a tarn. Continue north over another small hill to a craggy vantage point with good views of Coniston Old Man and the lake itself. The path drops down through bracken then descends between juniper bushes. When you reach a beck follow its course down for a few minutes, then fork left on a curving path and right at a junction which will take you to the shore of Coniston. The delightful path south through woods along the edge of the lake is in fact the Cumbria Way, the long-distance footpath from Carlisle to Ulverston. After about 1½ miles it rises towards the A5084. Turn right and return to the car park along the path on the verge. At a gentle pace the walk will take an hour and a half, but the lakeshore is a good place to dawdle and perhaps have a picnic.

☆ GRIZEDALE FOREST

This is a bewilderingly busy and exciting place in the heart of an ancient forest now managed and augmented by the Forestry Commission. There are 2,400 hectares of forest park, covering five miles of valley between Lake Coniston and Windermere, and criss-crossed by walks and mountain bike trails. The guide map on sale in the shop details a number of short walks and there's a separate guide for the Silurian Way, a $9^{1/2}$ -mile way-marked trail round the valley. You'll probably be lucky enough to see some of the red and roe deer and red squirrels that live here, but the badgers and foxes keep well away.

A sculptured wild boar in Grizedale Forest

The permanent exhibition in the centre tells the story of the forest - the monks who enclosed the coppice woods, the ancient industries of cooperage, basket weaving, and tanning, the charcoal 'bloomeries' for iron smelting, and the gunpowder mills. More recently, Grizedale Hall, which stood nearby and was demolished in 1956, was the site of the German PoW camp that features in the film *The One that Got Away*. It was from here that Luftwaffe ace Hans von Werra escaped before fleeing to Canada, across the frozen St Lawrence River to the US, and finally from Mexico back to Germany. He returned to flying and was killed soon afterwards.

What distinguishes Grizedale from similar forest visitors' centres is its size, and the other, arty activities that go on here - the sculpture project and the **Theatre in the Forest.** The theatre is a 220-seater which hosts drama, jazz and classical musical events from March to the end of December, mostly at weekends.

The **Sculpture in the Forest,** the work of both northern and international artists, adds a touch of magic to the forest walks. There are more than 75 sculptures, all 'site-related', which means they're made from materials from the forest itself, whether rock, timber or earth; the wild boars fashioned by Sally Matthews from twigs, leaves and mud are astonishing and magnificent. The **Gallery in the Forest** in the old sawmill has more sculpture on display and there's always an artist-in-residence in the attic gallery. A sculpture guide map is also on sale in the shop.

The Grizedale Forest Visitors' Centre is 3 miles south of Hawkshead on the road to Satterthwaite. Tel: 0229 860373. Theatre in the Forest box office: 0229 860291
Opening times: daily week before Easter-end Oct 10am-5pm; Nov, Dec, Feb, Mar weekends only; closed Jan. Times are subject to change. The walks and trails are accessible at all times
Admission: free
Grizedale Mountainbikes, by the Old Hall car park 50 yards beyond the centre, has bikes for hire for £12 per day, £7 per half-day

✪ HAWKSHEAD

This is easily the best of the Lake District's small towns, a pleasing confusion of narrow, tightly knit streets and 17th- and 18th-century buildings. Finding your way around, however, can be a bit confusing as they don't seem to have heard of street signs up this way. The best bet is to invest in a copy of the excellent illustrated town guide published by the National Park, available from the **Tourist Information Centre** in the main car park which is open daily April-October, weekends only in winter; tel: 05394 36525.

Hawkshead Grammar School, *alma mater* of William Wordsworth, is worth popping into, if only to see the great man's name carved on one of the desks. Judging by the amount of ancient graffiti, covering virtually every available wooden surface, these pupils did little else but deface school property. Wordsworth was a pupil here from 1779 till 1787, lodging locally. The school closed in 1909. One amusing exhibit, in a glass cabinet on the stairs, is an etiquette book from 1703 called *The Rules of Civility*, open at the following excerpt: 'You muft cut your Meat into fmall Pieces, and not put great Gobbets into your Mouth that may bunch out your Cheeks like a Monkey.'

Hawkshead Grammar School is opposite the Tourist Information Centre
Opening times: Easter-end Oct Mon-Sat 10am-12.30pm, 1.30-5pm; Sun 1-5pm; closes at 4.30pm in Oct
Admission: adult £1.50; child 50p

The **Parish Church** of St Michael and All Angels, on a hummock overlooking the town, is a peaceful old place with excellent views of Hawkshead and the countryside around. The 17th-century murals, with trompe l'oeil edging round the pillars, are striking, while the Celtic-style memorial to the war dead in the churchyard makes you wonder about the pagan proclivities of Hawkshead folk. To the north-west of the church, beyond the Town Hall, are a couple of interesting 18th-century buildings. Pillar Cottage has a jutting upper floor called a pentice supported by a pillar. Nearby, the spinning gallery is now the sole legacy of Hawkshead's wool trade.

The **Beatrix Potter Gallery**, the former solicitor's office of Potter's husband, is one of the big draws of the town. But on the basis that there is much in the fluffy bunny department yet to be endured, and in order to escape the crowds, time is better spent visiting a couple of ancient buildings beyond the town. The 15th-century **Courthouse** is all that's left of the manor buildings of Hawkshead, once owned by Furness Abbey. It is 10 minutes' walk north of the town up the B5286, immediately beyond the left turn to Coniston, but first you must get the key from the National Trust shop in Market Square (and pay a £5 deposit). Inside there's not much to see - wooden floors, rendered walls, a lovely tracery window - but it is thankfully silent and peaceful after the bustle of Hawkshead.

Colthouse to the east of the town, where Wordsworth probably lodged for at least some of his time at the grammar school, is a collection of old farmsteads and cottages. There is also a **Quaker Meeting House**, built in 1688, and containing some fine panelling. The key to it is available from Town End Farm a short distance south of Colthouse.

There are some decent cafés in Hawkshead, none better than the 15th-century **Minstrel's Gallery** in Flag Street, beyond the King's Arms and next to the Methodist Chapel. The original gallery is still in place, the floors are stone-flagged and the food is limited but wholesome and fresh - vegetable broth, toasted sandwiches, baked potatoes, and lots of cakes like chocolate and raisin brownies, coffee sponge and carrot cake. The Minstrel's Gallery is open mid-February to mid-December, 10.30am-5.30pm (closed Fridays).

At the south end of Hawkshead is **Esthwaite Water,** rather a dull lake flanked by two roads. There's a footpath to it at the south end of the village just where the road forks for Grizedale Forest. The lake is best known for being the setting of *The Tale of Mr Jeremy Fisher* by Beatrix Potter. Fishing permits and rowing boats for Esthwaite Water are available from Hawkshead Trout Farm, The Boat House, Ridding Wood, Hawkshead; tel: 05394 36541. Fishing costs £8.50 per day plus £7 for a boat; rowing boats cost £6.50 an hour.

☆ HOLKER HALL

Holker is a hike from the Coniston area, but worth it if you're a green-fingered car nut. The hall is the home of the Cavendish family, a branch of the Devonshires, and its highlights are the wonderful gardens and the Lakeland Motor Museum, owned and run separately from the hall. There are also a patchwork and quilting shop, an exhibition of Victorian, Edwardian and wartime kitchens, a craft and countryside exhibition, and the Clocktower café.

The wing open to the public was burnt down in 1871 and the replacement is a dog's breakfast of Victorian-Elizabethan in red sandstone. Queen Mary stayed here in 1937 to recover from the effects of the Abdication crisis, and her bathroom is interesting for being so primitive, rather like a shared facility in a 1950s boarding house. The most interesting room is the library, lined with 3,500 books including the works of scientist Henry Cavendish. His discovery of nitric acid is less interesting than the fact of his extraordinary misogyny. So hostile was he to women that he had a separate staircase built in his London house to prevent him ever setting eyes on the maids, and those who fell under his baleful stare were instantly dismissed. Funnily enough, he never married. A feature of the library is the false book spines, bearing spoof titles like *Nero on the Violin*, which hide the fuse boxes and light switches.

Holker benefits from the Gulf Stream and the gardens here are among the very finest in the country, covering 25 acres of forest, woodland and formal lawns, and including a rose garden, a blossom walk, a rhododendron and azalea walk, a wildflower meadow, and a flight of ornamental steps flanked by cascades. The mild climate and high rainfall carried from the Tropics are ideal for rare plants and shrubs like the ginkgo, and a 65-year-old azalea which flowered for the first time recently.

The **Lakeland Motor Museum** is situated in the old stables of the house. For access to the museum you have to pay admission to Holker Hall or gardens whether you want to see them or not, and on top of that pay a separate fee to enter the museum. But the exhaustive collection of close on 100 classic and vintage cars, motorbikes, jeeps, tractors, ambulances and boneshaker pedal bikes is impressive. There's also a collection of toy cars, and a re-creation of a 1920s garage.

Holker Hall is on the B5278, below the A590, a mile north of Cark. Tel: 05395 58328. Lakeland Motor Museum, tel: 05395 58509
Opening times: daily except Sat Apr 1-Oct 30, 10.30am-4.30pm (last admission, but gardens are open until 6pm)
Admission: house, grounds and Motor Museum - adult £5.25; child 6-16 £3; family ticket for up to 6 £14.50; grounds only - adult £2.75; child £1.55; Motor Museum - adult £1.50; child £1.30

☆ NEAR SAWREY

Hill Top in the heart of the village was Beatrix Potter's home from 1905 till her death here in 1943. If Hill Top stirs vague childhood memories, that's because the house, its gardens and the village of Near Sawrey featured throughout her books, and with remarkable fidelity. Through the gate opposite the house, for instance, is the rhubarb patch where Jemima Puddleduck spent much of her time. Stooping through the slate porch, you cross from *The Tale of Tom Kitten* into *The Tale of Samuel Whiskers*. The effect is rather disturbing. Like Potter's classic books, this 17th-century cottage somehow manages to be simultaneously small and grand, and it has a special and unmistakable feel. Beatrix Potter didn't simply knock off a few pretty pictures and stories that happened to hit the big time. She was a rare character - a superb draughtswoman, as her botanical illustrations and more serious watercolours show, a tireless worker on behalf of the National Trust, and an astute businesswoman. Hill Top is imbued with her spirit. 'First thing, when I come in on my own,' one of the guides said, 'it's not at all spooky - there's a lovely atmosphere to the house.' The guidebook contains some fascinating comparisons of her illustrations of house, gardens and village with contemporary photographs; it's interesting to go out and compare them for yourself.

Hill Top, Near Sawrey, on the B5285 2 miles south of Hawkshead. Tel: 05394 36269. There's a NT car park 200 yards north of the house
Opening times: Apr 1-Nov 1 11am-4.30pm (last admission) except Thurs, Fri. The NT shop, selling Potter knick-knacks, is open daily between the same dates 10am-5pm
Admission: adult £3.20; child £1.60; NT members free

Hill Top, Beatrix Potter's home in Near Sawrey

Close by Hill Top is the **Tower Bank Arms,** one of the few pubs owned by the National Trust, with its distinctive clock above the porch. The inn may feature in *The Tale of Jemima Puddleduck* but it wisely eschews furry animals or indeed any reference to Beatrix Potter. The bar is simple and unspoilt and there's a dining area and small garden for families as children are not allowed in the bar. Food is simple but good - salad and rolls, soup, plough-man's, specials such as steak and mushroom pie and lasagne, all available in children's portions. Its literary associations make the inn popular, so get there early to secure a table and expect delays as the staff get overworked. Food is served noon-2pm and 6.30-9pm every day (Sundays 7-9pm).

The Tower Bank Arms, as featured in The Tale of Jemima Puddleduck

☆ STOTT PARK BOBBIN MILL

The mill is a relic of Victorian industry - there were 64 bobbin mills in the Lakes in 1850 - so it seems amazing that Stott Park was operating as recently as 1971 when the age of plastic finally monopolised the manufacture of cotton bobbins, dufflecoat tog-gles and door wedges. Access to the mill is by guided tour only - and a very illuminating experience it is, for Stott Park is also a testament to Victorian working practices. There were no guards on the whirring belts and drill bits, smoking was allowed, and lighting was by paraffin lamps. As the guide said, this was 'a recipe for disaster'. Amid the blur of sawdust and shavings, as the machinery spewed out 100 gross bobbins every 10 hours, it is incredible that there was only one fatality in 136 years of opera-tion, though there were plenty of cases of scalps being ripped from skulls. Now it is just as well that the sound and fury of the machinery signifies little save the exquisitely turned souvenir bobbin each person takes away from the tour. This is a worthwhile visit, conducted by expert and humorous guides, providing an insight into a thankfully extinct way of working.

Stott Park Bobbin Mill is on the road running down the west shore of Windermere
about 7 miles south of Near Sawrey. Tel: 05395 31087
Opening times: daily Apr-end Sept 10am-6pm (or dusk if earlier)
Admission: adult £1.80; child 90p
There's a display on the history of Stott Park in the coppice barn next to the mill. An
informative English Heritage booklet is available for £1.45

 ## TARN HOWS

This squiggle of tarns, surrounded by grassy hillocks and fringed with trees, was created in the late 19th century as a landscape garden by the Marshall family of Monk Coniston Hall. They built a dam and flooded the valley to power a sawmill, planted pines, larches, oaks and spruces, and made a circular shoreline path. The result is one of the area's greatest beauty spots and attractions, a scaled-down, domesticated version of the real Lakeland. The walk round it is a leisurely flat dawdle of an hour or so, and there's even wheelchair access to its best viewpoint. We have Beatrix Potter to thank for being able to enjoy it today. She bought Tarn Hows in 1929 as part of the Monk Coniston estate, and sold it on to the National Trust. It gets terribly overrun though - erosion of soil and vegetation has become a major

The restored Victorian Stott Park Bobbin Mill

problem - and is best avoided in high season unless you go early in the morning. Apart from the shoreline walk it's worth climbing to the viewpoint on the eastern side to take in the views of the fells beyond, ranging from High Street to the Langdale Pikes.

Tarn Hows is a north turn off the B5285 between Hawkshead and Coniston. A one-way system operates on the access road.The NT car park charges £1 for parking. Boating is not allowed

Tarn Hows

⊛ ULVERSTON

Another one of these peripheral market towns, like Penrith and Cockermouth, Ulverston does its best to ignore the hustle and bustle of Lakeland tourism. Its main cobbled streets have an old-fashioned air about them and if you want to explore a bit the Tourist Information Centre has a leaflet of guided walks including one to the eccentric monument overlooking the town on Hoad Hill. Nicknamed 'the pepperpot', it is in fact a replica of the first Eddystone lighthouse and there are good views from up here of Morecambe Bay and the ship canal below. The Ulverston **Tourist Information Centre** is at Coronation Hall in County Square; tel: 0229 57120.

  Ulverston's claim to fame is as the birthplace of Stan Laurel, the thin soppy half of Laurel and Hardy. Stan was born Stanley Jefferson at 3 Argyle Street, Ulverston in 1890. In 1974, when

Ulverston's then mayor, Bill Cubin, unveiled a commemorative plaque on the house, it triggered an interest in Ollie and Stan that developed into an obsession. The result is the **Laurel and Hardy Museum**, tucked in a poky couple of rooms down a back alley near the centre of town. Bill Cubin is an amateur in the original and purest sense and his shrine to the bumbling duo is appropriately disorganised and eccentric, though plans are afoot to expand the museum and open a café.

Exhibits, which are most charitably described as eclectic, include 'Stan's personal ashtray', the stone cross from the spire of Stan's Sunday school, innumerable newspaper clippings, publicity shots, letters and showbills, the wooden toilet seat from Argyle Street, and a mangled bowler bearing the handwritten legend: 'Was this the hat Stan ate in Way Out West? (I doubt it!).' But the showpiece of the museum is the tiny cinema (the 32 pre-war seats are from a picture house in Accrington) showing Laurel and Hardy films on an endless loop. They made 105 films over 30 years, spanning the silent and sound eras, and Bill has copies of all but two (the prints of these have now been lost). Every half an hour or so, Bill stops the film to tell the story of 'two men who came together from very different worlds.' You can keep all your computer gadgetry and video presentations - this is the finest museum in the Lakes.

The Laurel and Hardy Museum, 4c Upper Brook Street, Ulverston. Tel: 0229 52292/861614
Opening times: daily 10am-4.30pm
Admission: adult £1; child 50p; family ticket for up to 5 £2

WHERE TO STAY

Coniston
⌂ ⚲6 🐎 ✉ £

Beech Tree Guest House, *Yewdale Road, Coniston, Cumbria LA21 8DB*
Tel: 05394 41717
Closed Jan
Owners John and Jean Watts had planned on semi-retirement when they moved from Cambridge to Coniston. They had reckoned without the hard work needed to restore

the village's derelict former rectory, in the shadow of Long Crag in the Yewdale Valley, into an exceptional (and exceptionally cheap) vegetarian guesthouse. It has been open six years now but work is still going on - the latest project is an ornamental vegetable garden to make Beech Tree virtually self-sufficient. The oldest part of the house dates from the late 1600s, there are rooms with and without bathrooms, all individually and comfortably decorated, a TV lounge and dining room. Evening meals are optional, but it would be a shame to miss out on John Watts' repertoire of 30 or so meat-free dishes, such as hummus or cashew nut pâté, baked mushroom, lentil and cheese slice, or red bean moussaka. Strictly no smoking.

Coniston
🏠 ᛉ10 ▭ ££

Coniston Lodge, *Sunny Brow, Coniston, Cumbria LA21 8HH*
Tel: 05394 41201
Open all year; R closed Sun & Mon
Built on stilts, the bedrooms of Coniston Lodge are antiseptically modern and give it the appearance of a motel. But don't let that put you off - inside it is top-notch, and there's a lot of history here too for an apparently recent building. The bedrooms have been grafted on to an older house, the one Donald Campbell was staying in at the time of his death. The Robinson family were friends of Campbell and let him stay there to avoid the Press. Now Anthony Robinson, who worked for Campbell, is the third generation of the family to become a Lakeland hotelier. The rooms he's had built are purposely larger than average - 'to keep the North Americans happy' - and each is named after a Lakeland tarn, with appropriate Heaton Cooper print hanging on the wall. The ample breakfasts and optional evening meals are taken in an unpretentious dining room in the old house, which features the steering wheel from one of the Campbell Bluebirds. No smoking.

Coniston
🏠 ᛉ ⱶ ▭ ££

Sun Hotel, *Coniston, Cumbria LA21 8HQ*
Tel: 05394 41248
Open all year
Another Campbell connection here - Donald stayed in the room on the corner with the bow window. The hotel was built at the turn of the century alongside the coaching inn that now serves as a pub. The Sun is a cheerful place with bright rooms in pale pinks, most of them with attached bathrooms. The lounge has comfy sofas and an open log fire, but the dining room is a lapse of taste - severely functional tables and chairs, cold blue decor. Both of them suffer from the view - whoever thought of obscuring the gardens by putting the car park in between should have his tyres let down. Last orders: bar food - lunch 2pm; dinner 9pm; restaurant - dinner 8.30pm.

Torver
🏠 ᛉ ⱶ ⌧ ££

The Old Rectory Country House Hotel, *Torver, Coniston, Cumbria LA21 8AX*
Tel: 05394 41353
Open all year
A turn off the A593 just north of Torver, this 19th-century rectory is set in three remote acres between the Coniston road and the shore of the lake. For the former abode of a Victorian clergyman it is remarkably light and airy. The rooms have Laura Ashley decor, floral arrangements, cane chairs, hair-dryers and mini-bars. Downstairs, the clean white restaurant tables look out through a conservatory extension on rolling countryside. Breakfasts are substantial and the four-course dinners

imaginative and good value - for instance, haddock smokies, pork fillet Normandy, home-made coconut and Malibu ice-cream, and cheeseboard. They cater for vegetarians too

if notified in advance. Lake Coniston is walkable from the hotel, and a sailing cruiser, *Spirit*, is available for hire to experienced sailors.

WHERE TO EAT

Coniston
🖼 ✕ 🗙 ££

Wheelgate Country House Hotel,
Little Arrow, nr Coniston
Tel: 05394 41418
Open mid-Mar - mid-Nov
Former medical receptionist Joan Lupton and husband Roger, a former financial consultant, upped sticks from Derbyshire to take over the Wheelgate, and they're determined to have fun. 'We do our own thing in our own way,' they say. 'We want to enjoy what we're doing or there's no point in doing it.' Though the Wheelgate is mainly a guesthouse, 'their own thing' also includes a simple but classy dinner menu and there's room for 6-8 non-residents (bookings only) in the beamed dining room. If you get there at 7pm there's time for a drink in the tiny bar, and coffee and truffles are served afterwards in the lounge. The menu offers only two choices per course - home-made soup or Morecambe Bay shrimps for instance, followed by haddock in cider or chicken and Stilton roulades, cheeses, and bread and butter pudding or Pavlova. The wine list is short but good.

Grizedale
🖼 ✕ 🍽 ££

Grizedale Lodge Hotel and Restaurant in the Forest, *nr*
Hawkshead
Tel: 05394 36532
Closed Christmas - mid-Feb
This is the place to come to for unrivalled Cumbrian fare, with a touch of Gallic *je ne sais quoi* thrown in. Margaret Lamb is a television cook who has had her own programme on Border TV. 'I try not to do things that other people do,' she says. 'You will never see a prawn cocktail or a black forest gâteau. My philosophy in food is true flavours. Sauces should enhance, not drown.' English and Cumbrian specialities include lamb in mead, 'Olde English style Beef and Wine Pie' and Grizedale venison, while she's equally at home turning out 'Hot Chicken Galatine with Walnut and Apricot Forcemeat'. Starters include fresh asparagus with garlic mayonnaise and apple and parsnip soup, puddings run to Yorkshire curd tart and crêpes suzette. The extensive, cheap wine list of 60 or so wines is notable for having a numbered system, with a full explanation of each at the back. It's just a pity that the restaurant is rather plain and severe. Dinner is served 7-8.30pm and you should reserve ahead.

Hawkshead
🏠 🍽 £

The Drunken Duck, *Barngates,*
nr Hawkshead
Tel: 05394 36347
Open all year
As it says in the brochure, the
Drunken Duck is 'on a crossroad in
the middle of nothing but magnificent scenery'. Indeed, finding it can
be a problem among a maze of minor
roads. Best bet is a left turn off the
B5286 a couple of miles north of
Hawkshead. There's a lovely old bar
- no jukebox or fruit machines -
where the menu is chalked up on a
blackboard, and food is ordered from
a counter in the middle of two
adjoining rooms (children are
allowed here though not in the bar).
The menu is exhaustive, ranging
from pastrami sandwiches, pâtés and
ploughman's to cottage pie, vegetable and butterbean casserole, and
coconut, lamb, ginger and lentil
curry. Puddings include syrup roly
poly and spotted dick. The food is of
superior standard for a pub, and the
surroundings earn high marks. Aside
from the hunting scenes (this is a
venue for the Coniston Hunt) there
are interesting old prints of Venice
and Dinan in France, and an intriguing billposter from 1693: 'To the
People of this Hamlet. Cast out all
Witches and Devils.' Perhaps this is a
clue to the runic cross in Hawkshead
churchyard. Last orders: lunch 2pm;
dinner 9pm. The Drunken Duck is
also residential.

Hawkshead
🏠 🍽 ££

Queen's Head Hotel, *Hawkshead*
Tel: 05394 36271
Open all year
A real find this - a pub-with-rooms
sort of place, in the centre of
Hawkshead, that just happens to
have one of the finest restaurants in
the area. They do bar food too, but
the dining room is a pleasure to eat
in and you can always start with a
drink in the bar. The dining room has
a French farmhouse look about it,
with beamed ceiling, dark panelling,
ornamental plates and cleverly
draped floral curtains. The menu
appears to cater for every conceiv-
able fancy but for once the quality
isn't sacrificed for range and quantity. It is probably best to eat simply
though, and stick with local and traditional dishes such as steaks, roast
Gressingham duck, Cumbria
supreme (pheasant) or local trout.
There's a good vegetarian choice too
- chilli, tagliatelle, and vegetable
bouchée, a selection of vegetables
cooked in cream and brandy. And if
you fancy a pot of mango tea, this is
the place. The restaurant is open
6.45-9.30pm every evening and all
day Sunday when traditional Sunday
lunches are served. Last orders for
bar food: lunch 2.30pm; dinner
9.30pm.

FELLWALKING

You haven't fully blooded yourself in the Lake District until you've climbed a fell or two. While the area has an infinity of wonderful low-level walks, there's nothing quite like getting up there on the roof of the world. When you've done it once the experience is likely to prove addictive - the perspectives are exhilarating and awesome, spiritual as well as geographical.

The Lake District boasts the four highest peaks in England - Scafell Pike (3,205 feet), Scafell (3,162 feet), Helvellyn (3,113 feet) and Skiddaw (3,053 feet) - as well as lots of lesser fells, such as the Langdale Pikes and the High Stile group, whose ascents are just as rewarding. While all of them can be climbed easily enough by reasonably fit walkers, you should be properly prepared and equipped.

This doesn't mean you have to kit yourself out like Chris Bonington, and beards, lumberjack shirts and plus-twos are no longer obligatory. But you need proper footwear - walking boots or stout shoes with ankle supports and grippy, not smooth, soles - and a lightweight but warm and waterproof jacket. Jeans or cords are not a good idea - they get heavy and clingy when it rains - and it's advisable to take a small rucksack with an extra jumper and waterproof overtrousers as it can get unbelievably cold and wet up on the tops.

You should also pack food, including high-energy stuff like chocolate and the local Kendal mintcake, something to drink, a torch, a whistle, a map and compass (but learn how to use them first) and a basic first aid kit. If you or someone in your group is injured and immobilised, the recognised SOS signal is six blasts on a whistle, or six torch flashes, every minute. A useful rule of thumb for gauging time and distance is to allow half an hour for every mile plus five minutes for every 30 metres of climbing (contours on Ordnance Survey maps are at 10-metre vertical intervals). Finally, always tell someone where you are staying of your intended route, and your estimated time of return.

WINDERMERE

Some 14 million people visit the Lake District every year - most of them seem to get no further than Lake Windermere and the A592 running up the eastern shore of the lake can be a nightmare. Windermere is the nearest the Lakes gets to a holiday resort and is a magnet for daytrippers and those for whom it is the only lake they have heard of.

Curiously for such a touristic mecca, its principal towns of Windermere and Bowness have little to offer. Kendal, some nine miles to the east, is a much better bet for shopping and browsing, with some good museums, a leisure centre and an arts centre. Halfway between Kendal and Windermere to the north of the A591 is the remote valley of Kentmere, the perfect antidote to the crowds and traffic jams. Another good alternative for beating the crowds is the maze of roads to the north of the Lyth Valley between Kendal and the lake. And the village of Cartmel to the south of Windermere makes an excellent excursion.

Still, Windermere became popular for a good reason and exploring it from the heights of Orrest Head, above Windermere town, or Gummer's Howe in the south will reveal the true beauty of this, the longest of the lakes, dotted with white boats and cradled by soft wooded fells. One begins to sympathise with Ruskin and Wordsworth, who feared that building the railway into Windermere would open a Pandora's Box of congestion and commercialisation. Then again, we're part of the problem too, whether we like it or not.

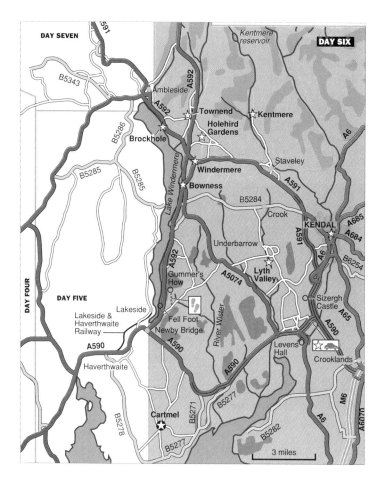

☆   BOWNESS

It's easy to be rude about Bowness-on-Windermere. It has all the charm of Blackpool on a Bank Holiday, which is fine if you enjoy being caught up in crowds of sweaty people trudging aimlessly about, queuing for ice-cream and swilling warm beer outside crowded pubs. But it does seem to miss the point of the Lake District. The town started life as a fishing village - its nucleus is in the jumble of old buildings called Lowside on the lake side of St Martin's church - but was subsumed into Windermere town in the tourist boom of the 19th century. Now the Promenade is one of the major departure points for the Windermere steamers, and the focal point for coach loads of day-trippers. The hideous complex of the Aquarius nightclub, shop and café on Glebe Road by the piers is a monument to its vulgarity.

The Bowness Bay Boating Co (05394 43360) operates sightseeing launches from Bowness along the middle section of Lake Windermere, and between Bowness Bay and Waterhead, Ambleside, throughout the year. From May 1 to Sept 30 launches leave Bowness for Ambleside every half hour 10am-5.30pm. From mid-May to mid-Sept there is also a regular service to Brockhole National Park Visitor Centre. Sample fares: 45-minute sightseeing tour £3; Bowness-Ambleside return £4

Round House, Belle Isle

Bowness itself is not all bad. The walk along Glebe Road to the headland called **Cockshott Point** offers good views of Lake Windermere and the curious round house on Belle Isle, still lived in by the Curwen family who have been there since 1776. There are another couple of good vantage points higher up behind the town - **Post Knott** and **Biskey Howe** - both detailed in another of the National Park's excellent guides available from the **National**
 Park Information Centre in Glebe Road just round the corner from the Promenade, which is open daily Easter-end October (tel: 05394-42895).

 The town has other worthwhile attractions, not least the **Old Laundry Visitor Centre** which has a theatre and exhibition hall and holds antiques and craft fairs, talks and outings throughout the year. But its centrepiece is the **World of Beatrix Potter** exhibition. There's a 10-minute introduction to the writer and her work, involving the ingenious, simultaneous use of nine video monitors, and then the door swings open on a magical model world re-created from Potter's books and characters. The dim lighting, dreamy music and exquisitely crafted tableaux weave an irresistible spell for children and adults alike - even the volubly cycnical teenagers I followed round subsided into grudging admiration. Set-pieces range from Jeremy Fisher's dinner with the tortoises to tiny colonies of mice buried in the bankside - and look out for the poacher's hands popping a bunny in the sack. The exhibition is rounded off by a 15-minute film in the theatre in which illustrations from the books are cleverly superimposed on photographs of the scenes as they are today.

The Old Laundry Visitor Centre is on the corner of Crag Brow and Rayrigg Road by the mini-roundabout. Tel: 05394 88444
World of Beatrix Potter opening times: Easter-end Sept 10am-7.30pm (last admission); Oct-Easter 10am-3.30pm (last admission)
Admission: adult £2.50; children £1.25

 There's no sleight of hand in the **Windermere Steamboat Museum**, but it's none the worse for that. The steam-driven yachts in which Victorians and Edwardians paraded themselves on Lake Windermere were lovely vessels, always referred to in the feminine. Now these elegant old ladies live out their days in the wet dock of the museum, their ensigns at rest bar the occasional sedate outing, their polished teak and brass gleaming as brightly as ever. Steam Launch *Dolly*, built in 1850, spent 67 years on the bottom of Ullswater before being rescued and restored. She is now the oldest mechanically powered boat in the world. The beautiful *Swallow*, from 1911, has all her original fittings including a kettle connected straight to the boiler which can boil a gallon of water in 10 seconds. TSSY *Esperance* was the model for Captain Flint's Houseboat in Arthur Ransome's children's classic, *Swallows and Amazons*. To walk round the gang-planks gazing down on the these sparkling old biddies is to understand something of the former glory of Windermere, long before the age of fibreglass cruisers and windsurfers. SL *Osprey* is taken out of mothballs to do 50-minute circuits of the lake, including cup of tea and biscuit - an opportunity not to be missed.

The permanent exhibition next to the wet dock tells the story of sailing on Windermere and includes the perfectly preserved hull from a yacht built in 1780, a demonstration of knot tying, and portraits of Windermere boating characters such as Old Oliver Haddock. There is also a shop, a café, a model boat pond and a nice picnic area with views north over the lake.

The Windermere Steamboat Museum is a few hundred yards north of Bowness centre on Rayrigg Road. Tel: 05394 45565
Opening times: daily Easter-end Oct 10am-5pm
Admission: adult £2.20; child £1.40; family ticket for up to 5 £5.80
Weather permitting, SL Osprey does 50-minute tours of the lake. Fares: adult £3.50; child £1.20

Sunset on Lake Windermere from Orrest Head

☆ BROCKHOLE

The Visitor Centre here is the hub and showcase of the Lake District National Park's activities. The house itself, built in 1900 by a silk merchant called William Gaddum, is a good example of the architecture of the arts and crafts movement. It was bought

Windermere Steamboat Museum, Bowness

by the National Park 24 years ago. The exhibition and film presentation tells the story of the Park, the growth of tourism and
the history of the Lake District, including the Norse derivations
of many local words - *dalr* (dale), *fjall* (fell), *bekkr* (beck), *tjorn*
(tarn). Throughout the season there are talks, demonstrations,
guided walks, and courses, all with an environmental emphasis
 and most of them specifically to do with the Lake District. The
restaurant and café serve hot food noon-2pm, and outside in the
gardens there's an adventure playground, activity trails, a cro-
quet and putting lawn, picnic area and shelter, a wildflower
meadow, and walks along the shore of Windermere. The jetty at
Brockhole is served by the Bowness Bay Boating Co. This is an
impressive and busy place where you'll learn a lot about the
Lake District and have fun at the same time.

Brockhole National Park Visitor Centre is on the A591 between Windermere town and
Ambleside. Tel: 05394 46601
Opening times: daily Apr, Sept, Oct 10am-5pm; daily May-Aug 10am-8pm
Admission: free, car parking charge £2
A comprehensive annual booklet, called 'National Park Events', has details of National
Park activities all over the Lakes with a section devoted exclusively to Brockhole. It is
available free from Tourist Information Centres or you can write to Brockhole for a
free copy

✪ CARTMEL

This delightful village is a bit off the beaten track, which is probably why it remains unspoilt and retains a strong sense of identity. It lies some ten miles south-east of the southern tip of Lake
Windermere, a minor turn off the A590 from Newby Bridge, and
should not be missed.

The grandly proportioned **Priory Church of St Mary and St**
Michael, with its diagonally set tower, stands benevolently over
the village. Theirs is an intimate association. During the
Dissolution the church survived because it served the parish as
well as the priory, while the monastery buildings were sacked
and the stones from them used to build the village. The fabric of
the church - mostly 13th-15th century - is impressive, but it's the
small-scale, human stories that are most engaging. Inside, below
the west window, is the grave of one Robert Harrison, drowned
'on Lancaster sand', Morecambe Bay, January 13 1780. Nearby

lies the body of his mother Margaret, drowned 'near the same place' in 1783, which is either a ghoulish coincidence or a case of the ultimate maternal self-sacrifice. In the graveyard there are more graves of sailors and walkers who died in the bay. Some of the stonemasonry is interesting too - several of the memorial slabs in the nave are carved with skull, crossbones and winged hourglass, symbolising death and the swiftness of passing time. And in a showcase is a rare copy of the 'Vinegar Bible' of 1716, so called because of a printer's error which rendered 'vineyard' as 'vinegar' (too much mead probably).

The only other relic of the monastery is the **Gatehouse,** the main entrance to the priory precinct, at the top end of the village square. It was built in about 1340 and is now owned by the National Trust and leased to George Jewell who runs Priory Fine Arts in the old courtroom on the first floor. The staircase is memorably dank and spooky and George is an engaging host. Unfortunately the secret underground passage linking the gatehouse with the priory church was blocked off in the 1920s when it was flooded by a stream.

The Gatehouse/Priory Fine Arts is open Apr-Oct Tues-Sun 11am-5pm; most afternoons in winter. Tel: 05395 36602
When the Gatehouse is closed George Jewell will come and open it up for you if he's at home: tel 05395 36691

Opposite the Gatehouse on the other side of the square is the **Antiquarian Bookshop** run by self-styled 'bibliopole' Peter Bain Smith and partner Leonie Park. This is just the ticket for whiling away a rainy afternoon - Peter's Rumpolesque figure, mazy conversations and garrulous erudition are guaranteed to make your visit amusing and informative. There are some 50,000 books here, including hundreds of first editions, stacked two and three deep on the shelves and in teetering piles on the floor. The shop specialises in local topography and children's books - there's a separate room for these, brimming with Arthur Ransomes and *Just Williams*. Open daily mid-February to mid-November 11am-6pm; winter 1-4.30pm, closed Monday and Tuesday; tel: 05395 36369.

Through the Gatehouse arch is the **Cavendish Arms**, the oldest of four pubs in the village. It may not be the prettiest from the outside, but tellingly it is the one favoured by the locals. Inside, the bar is sparsely furnished, with a separate restaurant area, but the menu is the same in both. There's a wide choice - the mammoth Cavendish open club sandwich (bacon, chicken lettuce, tomato and mayonnaise in toasted brown bread), steaks from the griddle, savoury pancakes such as chicken with pepper and tarragon, and unusual specials such as haggis and neeps, and dim sum. A friendly, buzzing place, especially at weekends. Children are allowed in the bar until 7.30pm.

 ## HOLEHIRD GARDENS

Here are the headquarters of the Lakeland Horticultural Society, in the midst of a delightfully varied garden on a slope above the north-east end of Lake Windermere. The house itself is a Cheshire Home for the chronically sick and disabled and is not open to the public. The estate comprises a walled garden, a heather garden, landscaped lawns with pools, fountains and cascades, and some good viewpoints across the lake to Langdale, Scafell and Coniston Old Man. Any time of year is impressive - in March, April and May there are azaleas, camellias, rhododendrons and daffodils; in summer lilies, hydrangeas, herbaceous borders and magnolias; in winter heather, snowdrops and witch hazel.

Holehird Gardens are off A592, the Kirkstone Pass road, just north of Troutbeck Bridge
Opening times: the gardens are always accessible
Admission: free

 ## KENDAL

A short hop from the M6, this bustling town is at the southern gateway to the lakes, and gets very busy despite the bypass. The one-way system devised to deal with the traffic can be frustrating, and though there is ample parking it is hard to find. Kendal got rich on the wool trade and still has an aura of prosperity about it. The main part of the town is on the west bank of the River Kent. On a hill to the east is the ruined castle, birthplace of Catherine Parr, the wife who outlived Henry VIII, and it's worth a stroll up for the view of the grey stone town huddled in the valley. The parish church is disproportionately wide - the nave is the second widest in the country - the result of additional building over the generations as the town, like the church, grew fat on the woollen trade. There's lots of history here, much of it housed in the town's three museums.

Abbott Hall Art Gallery and Museum of Lakeland Life and Industry is next door to the church. The exhibition on local life and work is housed in the former stable block to the main house. Though it has a reputation for being the finest of its kind in the Lakes, it has perhaps rested on its laurels for too long. It is desultory and slapdash, and renders the potentially interesting rather tedious. In the section on the woollen trade and weaving, you at least learn the derivation of the expression 'on tenterhooks' - tenters were frames used for stretching and drying cloth and the hooks were what you attached the cloth to. Further on, there is a 'typical' late 19th-century sitting room, a farmhouse kitchen from about 1770, a blacksmith's forge, a wheelwright, clogger and saddler, a collection of Victorian dolls - and a room devoted to that literary colossus, John Cunliffe, creator of Postman Pat and former Kendal schoolteacher. If you're interested in reading a file of his fanmail, fine. Arthur Ransome also gets a room to himself, which makes more sense. Adjacent to the craft shop is a collection of farming and veterinary implements which is, frankly, tedious.

The **Art Gallery** is much better. It is housed in Abbott Hall itself, a distinguished Georgian townhouse now filled with fine 18th-century furniture and art. There are several examples of the work of local lad George Romney - the painting of his teenage brother holding a candle is especially memorable. In the Ruskin Room there's a Turner watercolour, *The Passage of the St Gothard*, and upstairs an inspiring collection of 18th- and 19th-century 'picturesque' landscapes and sketchbooks of Lake District scenes, including works by Constable and Edward Lear. Contemporary art is represented by Kurt Schwitters, who lived in Ambleside, Ben Nicholson, and Elizabeth Frink.

Round the one-way system at the other end of town is the **Kendal Museum of Natural History and Archaeology**. Alfred Wainwright, exhaustive walker and writer on the Lake Disctrict, was Treasurer to Kendal Council 1948-67 and worked here as a curator. Many of the exhibits still bear his inimitable script and his cubby hole of an office is now an exhibit in itself - there are a pair of walking socks on the radiator, and a rucksack on the floor, as if primed for a quick getaway on a Friday night. The 'local' museum on the ground floor is a Victorian jumble of curios, from birds' eggs to animal traps and Egyptian artefacts. On the lower ground floor is the World Wildlife Gallery, a collection of stuffed animals divided up by continent. The Natural History Gallery upstairs is the best of the lot. It sets itself the modest task of telling 'the story of the Lake District from 520 million years ago' and presents reconstructions of a series of habitats between Kendal and the summit of Bowfell in Langdale - roadside verge, limestone wood, shore of Windermere, below the lake surface, up on the fell, and so on. The museum does an excellent series of worksheets for young children, such as the 'Creepy Crawly Trail'.

Abbott Hall Art Gallery and Museum of Lakeland Life and Industry is in Kirkland.
Tel: 0539 722464. Kendal Museum of Natural History and Archaeology is in
Station Road. Tel: 0539 721374
Opening times: late May - mid-Oct, 10.30am-5pm Mon-Sat, 2-5pm Sun; reduced
hours the rest of the year
Admission: one museum only - adult £2; child £1. Art Gallery and Museum of
Lakeland Life and Industry - adult £3; child £1.50. All three museums - adult £4; child
£2; family ticket £10

'What is thoroughly English and truly representative of England? Chocolate of course.' So says Joy - 'just Joy' - proprietress (high priestess too) of **1657 The Chocolate House**, 'the only chocolate house in the country'. 1657 is apparently when England's first chocolate house opened, and only England had them because the Pope banned them everywhere else. Now Joy has revived the tradition in a higgledy-piggledy mediaeval cottage as 'a 100 percent English attraction' - all the 'serving wenches' have to have been born in England ('whatever their colour or creed') and you'll find only authentic 17th-century chocolate house fare on the menu. There are no sandwiches ('there was no Earl of Sandwich in 1657'), no condiments ('because they didn't exist'), just a queasy range of chocolate-based goodies, from 26 sorts of drinking chocolate to sweets, mousses and cakes. Varieties, in liquid or solid form, include Catherine of Braganza, Old Noll (Cromwell's nickname), Minette (Charles II's sister), and Aztec, topped with 24 carat gold leaf. Bizarre.

1657 The Chocolate House is on the cobbled Branthwaite Brow between Market Square
and Finkle Street. Tel: 0539 740702
Opening times: 9am-5.30pm Mon-Sat; early June-Oct half-term also open Sun

For some real food visit the **Brewery Café and Restaurant** in the Brewery Arts Centre off Highgate, which offers sustenance for the soul as well as the stomach. The café is part of an open-plan arrangement of cinema, theatre, workshops and galleries. There's a good selection of salads and open sandwiches, a hot dish of the day such as steak and kidney pie, a children's menu, and home-made cakes and puddings and herb teas. You can eat at the café tables, surrounded by paintings, or take food next door to Vats Bar, where the giant brewery vats have been segmented to form discreet drinking bays. There's also a terrace for summer eating. Open Monday-Saturday 9.30am-7.30pm.

☆ KENDAL CASTLES DRIVE

South of Kendal are a couple of castles that can be taken in on the same trip. Take the A6 from the town centre. This presently joins the A591. Take the A590 at the major junction and pick up the A6 again after half a mile. **Levens Hall** is another mile south beyond a junction. This mediaeval and Elizabethan manor

Weird and wonderful shapes in Levens Hall's topiary garden

house, which has been in the Bagot family for 700 years, is hand-some enough. It has Jacobean furniture, plasterwork ceilings, and an interesting collection of early 19th-century watercolours by Peter de Wint, in a rare state of preservation because they were hidden away for many years. But what sets Levens apart from other stately piles is the extraordinary topiary garden, designed in 1689 and completed in 1720. The yew, golden yew and box trees that comprise it are sculpted into a fantasmagoria of shapes - birds, Heath Robinson teapots, umbrellas, spirals, and other forms that defy description. If there were an earthly wonderland for Alice to inhabit, this would be it. There's also a good example of a 'ha ha', a popular 18th-century landscape device. It consists of a ditch and bank between the gardens and the pasture land which create the illusion of continuity between the two, whilst preventing cattle from wandering into the gardens.

Levens Hall is five miles south of Kendal on the A6. Tel: 05395 60321
Opening times: Easter Sun-end Sept, Sun-Thurs 11am-5pm (last admission to house 4.30pm)
Admission: house and gardens - adult £3.50; child £1.90; family ticket for up to 4 £10; gardens only - adult £2.20; child £1.10; family ticket £6

Back towards Kendal, **Sizergh Castle**, owned by the National Trust, is a left turn just before the major junction of the A590 and the A591. The 60 foot pele tower is the biggest in Cumbria, and the most interesting part of the house to walk round. Since it was built in the 14th century there have been additions of a Tudor hall and two Elizabethan wings, which makes Sizergh pretty interesting architecturally. Inside is the usual agglomeration of old furniture, carved woodwork, panelling and what have you, though nothing in truth is very startling. The gardens feature an ornamental lake, on the far side of which is the best view of the house, reflected in the still waters. Unfortunately the tranquillity of the place is spoilt by the constant noise of traffic on the nearby A591. There are a number of walks around the Sizergh estate, which covers nearly 1600 acres and includes the ancient woodlands of Brigsteer.

Sizergh Castle. Tel: 05395 60070
Opening times: Apr-Oct, grounds - 12.30-5.30pm, castle - 1.30-5pm
Admission: house and grounds - adult £3.10; child £1.60; gardens only - adult £1.60; child 80p; NT members free

☆ KENTMERE

The perfect way to re-acquaint yourself with the unspoilt natural beauty of the Lakes after the congestion of Windermere. The village of Kentmere is four miles beyond Staveley, a turn off the A591 between Kendal and Windermere, and the road up to it follows the course of the River Kent which has its source up in the bleak rocky heights surrounding Kentmere reservoir. From the village the road climbs steeply for another mile before petering out by a couple of farms. From here it's more than two miles' rugged walking, past a ruined house and the sheer outcrop and scree slopes of Rainsborrow Crag, to the reservoir, in the shadow of Ill Bell. (The bridleway off to the right before the ruined house is the Nan Bield Pass which will take you via Small Water tarn into Haweswater).

☆ LYTH VALLEY

The minor roads between Windermere and Kendal - the B5284 via Crook, or the road which starts at the southern end of the lake and goes through Crosthwaite and Underbarrow - are reasonably quiet and take in some lovely countryside above the Lyth Valley. On the road between Underbarrow and Kendal is a car park serving the beauty spot of Underbarrow, or Scout Scar. Follow the footpath on the other side of the road along the edge of this limestone precipice. The views from the southern end, especially, are breathtaking: ahead Coniston Old Man, the Langdales and the Scafells; to the south Morecambe Bay.

Back down the road towards the southern tip of Windermere, wedged into a shelf of fellside where two roads join, is the **Masons Arms** at Strawberry Bank. The *Los Angeles Times*, no less, extols the virtues of this classic English pub over such staple tourist attractions as Big Ben - and with good reason. The setting, overlooking the valley of the River Wister, is superb (especially if you can get a table on the terrace), the interior quaintly rustic, and the range of beers exhaustive. As well as bitters brewed on the premises there are 200 bottled brews on offer, from Polish Okocim to Rhino from Namibia. The menu tries a bit too hard to be similarly global, and your best bet is to stick with local dishes such as coachman's casserole (beef in red wine with chestnuts, mushrooms and shallots), or a salad. Food is served every day noon-2pm and 6-8.45pm. Children are allowed in the bar until 9.30pm. It's advisable to get there early as parking is limited.

Farmhouse in the Wister Valley

TOWNEND, TROUTBECK

This is a prime example of a 17th-century yeoman farmer's dwelling, with its characteristically fat cylindrical chimney stacks and oak mullioned windows. There are other good examples in the Lake District, but none has Townend's wealth of original detail inside. Until the National Trust took it over in 1947, Townend had been in the same family, the Brownes, since the late 16th century. A combination of the family's reluctance to modernise, and their apparently genetic aptitude at wood carving, has left us with a time capsule of dark, panelled rooms and hand-carved furniture - beds, cupboards, trunks, tables and chairs. Many pieces bear the date when they were made, as if successive generations of Brownes anticipated the time when their home would become a museum piece and obligingly catalogued its contents in advance.

Townend is 3 miles north of Windermere town, at the south end of Troutbeck between the A591 and the A592. Tel: 05394 32628
Opening times: Apr 1-Nov 1, 1-4.30pm, or dusk if earlier; closed Sat & Mon
Admission: adult £2.30; child £1.20; NT members free

The Swan steamer plying Lake Windermere

☆ WINDERMERE TOWN AND LAKE

The town of Windermere is a non-place really. It has shooed most of the undesirable elements of mass tourism - the car parks, gift shops and cafés - down to Bowness, built a one-way system that keeps the traffic moving, and retreated behind its façades of prim Victorian and Edwardian villas, most of them guesthouses. The **Tourist Information Centre**, on the corner of Victoria Street and the A591, next to the station, is one of the best in the Lakes, very helpful and almost always open (tel: 05394 46499).

WINDERMERE VIEW POINTS WALK

A short walk from the Information Centre - take the path on the other side of the A591 opposite the National Westminster Bank - leads you to **Orrest Head**, one of the very best vantage points over Lake Windermere. It's a well trodden path and the final ascent to the summit has been re-routed because of erosion, but you can see why people make the effort - the lake below, behind it the Langdale peaks and the Coniston fells, to the north the gentle hills around Grasmere, are all spread magically at your feet. Too often, though, the visibility is poor. For maximum effect try it on a clear evening, when the fells are backlit by the dying sun and the lake and forests on the far shore shimmer in haze.

At the other end of the lake is **Gummer's How**, another beauty spot with equally arresting aerial views. About a mile north of Newby Bridge take the minor road branching sharply uphill from the A592 opposite Fell Foot Country Park. Just before the second steep incline is a car park and picnic area on the right hand side. Park here and walk up through the woods for 50 yards before turning left and crossing the road. Follow the path opposite which will take you to the summit. The final ascent up a rocky path strewn with boulders can be avoided by following the path to the right which curves round more gently to the top. Up here is a grassy plateau criss-crossed with paths, an ideal spot for a picnic if it's not too windy. The views back up the lake are spectacular.

At the junction with the A592 at the base of the lake is **Fell Foot Country Park**, a National Trust park of grassy picnic areas, a sloping beach where swimming is reasonably safe, an adventure playground, the Boathouse Café and information centre, rowing boat hire, and launching for dinghies and powered boats of less than 5 hp. There's plenty of car parking and the grounds are open all year, the facilities only in season.

Fell Foot car park is open 10am-dusk all year round. From the week before Easter-end Oct, when facilities are open, there are charges for parking. Rowing boats are available for hire for £5 an hour for two people
From Fell Foot there is also a steamboat ferry called Cygnet that plies between the park and Lakeside, 50p one way

Lakeside, on the western shore at the southern tip of the lake, is the major departure point for the Windermere steamers. The Windermere Iron Steam Boat Company operates three large passenger ships, the *Swan, Teal* and *Tern*, which ply the length of the lake nine times a day at the height of the season. The recently refurbished vessels all have open decks, covered saloons, coffee lounge and licensed bar. The return journey takes just over three hours. There are two stopping points, Bowness and Waterhead (Ambleside), which are also alternative points of embarkation.

Too many people think that visiting Windermere and not sailing on the lake is an omission on a par with going to Rome and missing the Colosseum, and these lake trips are easily Cumbria's top tourist attraction. The boats get so crowded that the experience is faintly humiliating and little different from a cross-Channel ferry. This feeling is reinforced if you take up the optional part of the trip, the short journey on the **Lakeside & Haverthwaite Railway**. The scenery is extremely pleasant, and manages to be very varied in the course of three and a half miles - a tunnel and a deep rock cutting, waterfalls, pastures and forests in the Leven Valley, the edge of the lake itself. And the steam locos are engaging, wheezing old gents. But the carriages - standard British Rail circa 1972 despite their maroon and cream livery - and the hordes of passengers are reminiscent of the Dover boat train. This is a trip to be approached with caution, and probably only attempted on quiet days.

Windermere Iron Steamboat Company is at Lakeside, Newby Bridge. Tel: 05395 31188
Operating times: early Apr-Nov 1
Sample fares: Lakeside-Waterhead return - adult £7; child £3.50
Lakeside & Haverthwaite Railway Co Ltd is at Haverthwaite Station. Tel: 05395 31594
Operating times: daily 2 wks either side of Easter and early May-Nov 1
Fares: Haverthwaite-Lakeside return - adult £2.65; child £1.35

WHERE TO STAY

Bowness
👜 🕴 🖂 £

Laurel Cottage, *St Martin's Square, Bowness, Cumbria LA23 3EF*
Tel: 05394 45594
Open all year
Facing the church in the old and nicest bit of Bowness, Laurel Cottage dates from 1613. It was built to be the old grammar school, by public subscription, and was the first house in Bowness to have wooden floors. Quaint as it is, there looks to be scarcely room to swing a cat from the outside. Appearances are deceptive - inside, the cottage has been knocked through to the former flat of the manager of Barclays Bank next door, and the rooms here are large, including two family rooms, all with TV. If it's atmosphere you want, stick with the old cottage rooms, with their low ceilings and crooked doors, but the walls are thin and there is therefore no TV.

Bowness
🛏 🕴 🖛 £££

Linthwaite House Hotel, *Crook Road, Bowness, Cumbria LA23 3JA*
Tel: 05394 88600
Open all year except Christmas
This former private house, set in 15 acres and with cracking views over Lake Windermere, was built in 1900 and in the last few years has been systematically 'de-modernised' by owner Mike Bevans. The result is reassuringly Edwardian without being gloomy. Downstairs the softly lit nooks and crannies are offset by the lightness of the new conservatory, while the 18 bedrooms are lavishly and individually decorated, all with satellite TV, and some with canopied beds. It's far from being precious, though. Service is friendly and informal and the genial owner is always on hand. Linthwaite House is on the B5284 about a mile out of Bowness.

Cartmel
sc ⅋ 🐕 🛏 £££

Longlands, *Cartmel,*
Cumbria LA11 6HG
Tel: 05395 36475
Open all year

'Longlands at Cartmel is a special place for those who enjoy undisturbed peace and tranquillity', says the sign on the entrance gates. This Georgian country house set in rolling acres a mile north of Cartmel village is as good as its word. Robert and Judy Johnson gave up the rat-race to create at Longlands superior holiday accommodation with a rare ambience of luxury and peace. The eight cottages were converted from outhouses and are grouped round a secluded courtyard at the rear of the house. They retain the original stonework, timbers and features - the Old Kitchen still has hooks in the ceiling for hanging pots and pans - but are now fitted out to the highest standards and furnished with uncluttered elegance. All are double-glazed and centrally heated and have microwaves and dishwashers, TV, and baths as well as showers. In the grounds there's a walled garden for catching the sun - the climate down here is far better than elsewhere in the Lakes, courtesy of the Gulf Stream - and a herb garden for the use of guests. And on Friday and Saturday nights from May to October Robert Johnson puts on his pinny and knocks up delicious five-course meals that are served in the dining room of the main house.

Crooklands
sc ⅋ 🛏 ££

Millness Hill Country Park,
Crooklands, nr Kendal, Cumbria
Tel: 0502 500500 (for bookings)

Open all year

These timber lodges are scarcely in the middle of nowhere - just a screen of trees separates them from the M6 at the very south-east extremity of the Lakes - but they are handy for the motorway and the park includes an attractive stretch of the Lancaster Canal (a rowing boat is available for use). There are three sizes and prices of accommodation. All lodges have TV and video recorders, microwaves and fridge freezers, showers, double glazing and central heating, and the smarter ones have mirrored whirlpool baths so you can pretend you're Joan Collins.

Windermere
G ⅋12 🛏 ££

The Archway Country Guest House,
13 College Road, Windermere, Cumbria
Tel: 05394 45613
Open all year

For people who take their brains with them on holiday, the Archway near Windermere town centre is a bookish and arty place. It has unusual prints on the walls (Edvard Munch, and framed leaves from a Victorian guide to the Old Masters), artfully scattered literary biographies and classics and a pleasantly thoughtful atmosphere. There are six rooms, all with TV, telephone, home-made biscuits, Victorian bedspreads and little libraries of novels and poetry anthologies. The rooms at the front have good views across the trees to Coniston Old Man and the Langdale peaks and the small single room in the attic is cut-off and womb-like with the feel of a tree house. Owner Aurea Greenhalgh makes all her own bread, juices, yoghurt and preserves, and most of the meat, poultry and eggs is from an organic farm in Yorkshire. Evening meals are confined to two courses to keep the price down. Strictly no smoking.

Windermere
🏠 ⅄ 🚇 £££
Merewood Country House Hotel,
Ecclerigg, Windermere,
Cumbria LA23 1LH
Tel: 05394 46484
Open all year
You'd best pack your best bib and tucker if you're planning on staying in this former home of the Earl of Lonsdale. One of the highlights of Merewood is the Saturday night dinner-dance in the grand Lonsdale Suite. Everything about Merewood is grand - hand-made marble floors, leather sofas, original fireplaces with open fires, chandeliers, and the view from the 20 acres of landscaped gardens overlooking the north end of Lake Windermere. The 20 rooms (named, predictably enough, after writers) are ridiculously large, done out in regulation Laura Ashley, some with four-posters and half-tester beds, all with telephone and TV. A sumptuous experience, even if you feel the 'grandness' is just a teeny bit forced. Merewood is off the A591 between Windermere town and Ambleside, just past the entrance to the Brockhole National Park Visitor Centre.

WHERE TO EAT

Bowness
✕ 🚇 ££
Jackson's Bistro, *St Martin's Place,*
Bowness
Tel: 05394 46264
Closed Sun in winter
A Cole Porter classic plays quietly in the background. The atmosphere is dark and discreet. Frank Jackson, a former catering lecturer from Manchester, opened his bistro eight years ago after running a country house hotel for 10 years. Ask for a table in the candlelit cellar room with its beamed ceiling and old range, choose a bottle from the unsnobbish wine list (it has a guide to sweetness and fullness) and enjoy starters like Greek island salad, or grilled lamb's kidneys with smoked bacon; main courses such as beefsteak and mushroom casserole braised in Guinness, seafood mornay, or (for those who haven't eaten in a week) Jackson's Special Grill: steak, lamb chop, pork fillet and Cumberland ham in mustard sauce. Last orders for dinner 10.30pm.

Bowness
✕ 🚇 £££
The Porthole Eating House,
3 Ash Street, Bowness
Tel: 05394 42793
Closed Mid-Dec - mid-Feb & Tues
No one does it quite like the Italians. Surely the finest restaurant in the Lakes, the Porthole is a memorable experience not just for the food, perfect as it is, but for the consummate front-of-house style of owner Gianni Berton, who makes you simply glad to be alive and enjoying your food and wine. The quote from Byron on the chimney breast says it all: 'Let us have wine & women, Mirth and laughter, Sermons and soda water The day after.' Although he no

longer takes day-to-day charge in the kitchen, Gianni continues to devise and experiment with new dishes. The menu combines classic Italian, French and English food with a touch of nouvelle cuisine. Gianni uses his mother's Venetian recipes, while the typically Tuscan dishes are courtesy of his Aunt Ancilla in Lucca. The wine list is excellent. If the weather is halfway decent, ask to eat upstairs in the patio garden - it will take little imagination to fancy yourself in Tuscany. Booking is strongly advised. Last orders for dinner 10.30pm.

Cartmel
🏠 ✕ 🍴 **£££**
Uplands Country House Hotel,
Haggs Lane, Cartmel
Tel: 05395 36248
Closed Jan 1-Feb 22 & Mon
Owners Diana and Tom Peter learned the ropes under John Tovey at the renowned Miller Howe in Windermere before opening Uplands in 1985. Tom's nouvellish cooking is matched by the airy pastel decor, Impressionist prints and posters, and Rolls-Royce service - almost silent but powerfully efficient. A different, limited choice four-course menu every night might include hot salmon soufflé wrapped in smoked salmon with watercress sauce, a tureen of fennel and almond soup, baked fillet of sea bass with chives and Noilly Prat sauce, and home-made passion fruit ice cream in a brandy snap basket.

Uplands is a left turn opposite the Pig and Whistle in Cartmel village, at the top of the hill on the left-hand side. Dinner is 7.30 for 8pm.

Windermere
✕ 🍴 **£££**
Roger's Restaurant, *4 High Street, Windermere*
Tel: 05394 44954
Dinner only
The Roger in question being Roger Pergl-Wilson and wife Alena, who've been here for more than decade now, and in that time established a restaurant of national renown - the Windermere area really has an embarrassment of high class eateries. Outside it is flower-decked, inside there are two eating areas (ask for a table upstairs) with dark wallpaper and fabrics, candles and flowers on the tables. The emphasis is on French cuisine - Roger holds special French provincial cookery evenings - blended with local dishes and Roger's own way with sauces and presentation. Though he isn't a crusader for organic food, he avoids using meat from factory farms. One of his local delicacies is Windermere char, in a mousseline as a starter, or filleted in flaky pastry and prawn sauce as a main course. This disappears fast, so be there early to make sure it's still on the menu. Booking, especially on Fridays and Saturdays, is essential. Last orders for dinner 9.30pm.

THE WORDSWORTH CONNECTION

The literary pilgrimage may not be top of everyone's holiday agenda, but understanding a bit about Wordsworth and the other Romantics can give a fresh perspective on the Lakes.

Born in Cockermouth, Wordsworth had unhappy stays in Penrith, went to school in Hawkshead, and lived in Grasmere and Rydal. An addicted walker, he also devoured thousands of miles of Lakeland fells during his lifetime and wrote many more words on the people and landscape he loved.

Wordsworth broke the mould of high-falutin poetic style by daring to write about 'incidents and situations from common life' - about peasants, recluses, madmen and outcasts who lived and died locally - in 'language really used by men'. He also expressed the true, sometimes frightening splendour of the fells and lakes, most memorably in *The Prelude*.

During the early 19th century the whole of Wordsworth's hippy-ish circle lived and loved in each other's pockets. Wordsworth himself lived at Dove Cottage with wife Mary and sister Dorothy. Mr and Mrs Coleridge lived up the road at Keswick with Poet Laureate Robert Southey and his wife Edith, who was Mrs Coleridge's sister. And to further complicate matters, Coleridge was forever sloping off to Dove Cottage for trysts with Mrs Wordsworth's sister, Sara Hutchinson.

The journals Dorothy kept during these years reveal the debt of Wordsworth's poetry to her acute observations of nature. The journals also read as if the intervening 200 years had never been - the walks, plants, and views Dorothy wrote about are still there, and it's not hard to summon a picture of Wordsworth or Coleridge mooning about o'er hill and down dale.

The most vivid portrait of Wordsworth himself is by Thomas De Quincey, who took over the lease of Dove Cottage when the Wordsworths moved out. 'Useful as they have proved themselves,' he wrote in one memorable passage, 'the Wordsworthian legs were certainly not ornamental; and it was really a pity, as I agreed with a lady in thinking, that he had not another pair for evening dress parties.' If you meet a fellwalker with dodgy legs babbling about daffodils, you'll know who he is.

GRASMERE

The geographical and spiritual heartland of the Lakes, Grasmere and its environs are dense with fascinating walks and places to see and visit. If you have studiously avoided Wordsworth so far, this is where the great man catches up with you with a vengeance. In any case it's best to go with the flow, not least because a proper appreciation of the Lake District is incomplete without an understanding of Wordsworth & Co.

Grasmere is where the Lake District as we know it, the tourist destination, began. The painters who came here in the late 18th century, the early guidebook writers, and the poetry of Wordsworth, all paved the way for the tourist boom which has never looked back since the middle of the 19th century. If you visit just one museum during your stay in the Lakes, make it the Wordsworth Museum next to Dove Cottage, which explains this evolution better than anywhere else.

The lovely small lakes of Rydal Water and Grasmere are best appreciated on a leisurely circular walk which passes Grasmere church and village, Dove Cottage, and Rydal Mount. Just down the road is Ambleside, one of the liveliest towns in the Lake District, with more to it than meets the eye from a car window. And out to the east is arguably the Lake District's most impressive valley, Great Langdale, whose distinctive twin Pikes are visible from just about everywhere in central Lakeland. More than any other physical feature, these brooding peaks sum up the mystery and majesty of the Lake District.

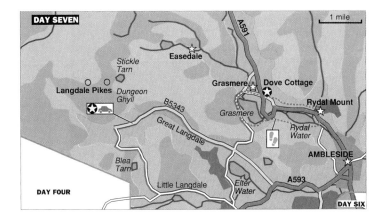

☆ AMBLESIDE

This is one of the busiest towns in the Lakes, so we shouldn't complain too much about the one-way system, which can make it feel like the central reservation of a roundabout but mercifully keeps the traffic flowing. Ambleside also suffers from not having a focus - the mediaeval village was at the north end in the cluster of streets around Chapel Hill, while the southward Victorian expansion reached as far as Waterhead, at the northern tip of Lake Windermere, after the first regular steamer service began running to Newby Bridge in 1845. Because the lay-out is rather confusing it is easy to miss some of the better features and come away with an impression that doesn't do Ambleside justice. The National Park leaflet on the town, available from the **Tourist Information Centres** in Ambleside or Waterhead, has a good map and photographs and a potted history that puts you in the picture. Ambleside TIC, in the Old Courthouse, Church Street (tel: 05394 32582), is open daily April-October, weekends only in winter.

Waterhead has a car park with the TIC (tel: 05394 32729), a pier and launch sites for boats, a café, and a scattering of shops. There's also Borrans Park, just beyond the Wateredge Hotel, where there's a pleasant lakeshore walk past small beaches and decent views across Windermere, especially from a rocky promontory planted with Scots pines. Beyond it, at the confluence of the Rivers Brathay and Rothay, is Galava Roman fort, first established in 79AD as a wooden structure and rebuilt in stone in 120AD under the Emperor Hadrian. Two gates and towers, the commandant's house, the headquarters and granaries are laid out in a grid pattern in the centre of a field. Notice to the north by the roadside a lovely old, typically Lakeland barn.

Ambleside - A typical Lakeland barn and the two-room Bridge House

Hire boats are available at Waterhead from Easter until the end of October, depending on the weather. Rowing boats cost from £2.20 an hour; open top motor boats from £6.50 per hour; cabin cruisers from £9 an hour. There's a minibus service into Ambleside than runs 10am-5.30pm daily in season and costs 60p. **Horse and trap tours** into Ambleside run every 20 minutes noon-5pm daily in season and cost 75p one-way.

Another pleasant walk is to be had in **Rothay Park**, beyond the parish church of St Mary's. Just where the one-way system turns sharp right up Compston Road continue straight ahead past the tennis courts and park by the church itself. Follow the path to the park past an infants' school. There's an adventure playground (for under-13s only), picnic tables and paths alongside the River Rothay and Stockghyll. Where the two streams meet is a packhorse bridge called Miller Bridge, on the old route to Langdale.

Running north-east from the bridge on the course of the old route is a path that takes you to the A591 at the north end of Ambleside. The 'Italianate' villa on the left, called the Knoll, was built by a social reformer and feminist called Harriet Martineau in 1846.

The top end of the town is where you'll find the tourists thickest on the ground. The car park is here, and a tatty agglomeration of cafés and trinket shops. One of the biggest draws is the curious **Bridge House**, a two-room Lilliputian building straddling Stockghyll where it runs parallel with the main through road. Now a National Trust information centre, the building dates from the 17th century and served as a summer house for the vanished Ambleside Hall. Here the hordes swarm on the pavement and pose for snapshots, while across the road some of the most architecturally interesting bits of Ambleside remain deserted. **Smithy Brow, Chapel Hill** and **North Road** are all worth wandering through for a sense of the atmosphere of the old village.

When the Victorians started coming in serious numbers in the 1840s, Ambleside's most famous beauty spot was **Stockghyll Force**, a 70-foot waterfall to the east of the town centre. To reach it take the road off Lake Road (the A591) next to Barclays Bank. There's a parking spot about half a mile up, across the gorge from a lovely old bobbin mill now converted into holiday flats. You can see why the waterfall was - and still is - so popular. The deciduous woods that once provided the raw material for the bobbin mill are delightfully shady, the ascent to the falls is gentle, and the view, from a railed vantage point, satisfyingly precipitous.

✪ DOVE COTTAGE

Aided and abetted by Samuel Taylor Coleridge, Wordsworth produced some of the most memorable poetry in the English language - including *Ode: Intimations of Immortality, Resolution and Independence* and *The Prelude* - during the few heady years he spent here in the early 19th century. Dove Cottage really hasn't changed that much since the Wordsworths handed over the lease to Thomas De Quincey in 1808, apart, that is, from the hundreds of thousands of visitors who beat a path to its door every year.

Dove Cottage, home to the Wordsworths then Thomas De Quincey

The downstairs is still panelled from when it was a pub (the Dove and Olive Bough) in the 18th century. The kitchen utensils and furniture have an air of recent use about them. The dia-mond-shaped chair with curved support in which Wordsworth would sit composing - his back resting on one side, his notebook on the other - begs to be sat in (but you're not allowed, so don't). And the human details really bring the place alive - the guide tells how Coleridge would sleep in front of the hearth in the study while De Quincey kipped down in the woodshed, and that the perfectly circular mark burnt into the wooden floorboards of the landing is where De Quincey left a bucket of burning coals, no doubt after over-indulging in the local preparation of opium known as Kendal Black Drop. A phial of this stuff, three times stronger than your standard issue laudanum, sits in one of the display cabinets alongside Wordsworth's John Lennon-type sun-glasses.

From the outside the cottage could belong to Benjamin Bunny or Tom Kitten. The white, lime-washed walls and small lattice win-dows are immediately recognisable from the earliest known painting of the cottage, on display in the **Wordsworth Museum** next door. The museum is superbly done. It explains the origins of the Romantic movement in poetry and art, of which the lake and fells of Grasmere were the cradle, and which was responsible for the term 'picturesque'. The early landscape painters had terrible problems with perspective, preferring to soften and foreshorten the crags for fear of giving offence by presenting untamed nature. One of their favourite tools was a Claude Glass, a convex mirror used to 'compose' the landscape in a viewfinder. Wordsworth, meanwhile, was breaking new ground in poetry by showing that 'delicacy and depth of feeling are not limited to any one class of men and women'. There are recorded readings from *The Prelude* available on headphones. The passage dealing with his father's death, and the lines on stealing a skiff on Ullswater, accompanied by a painting of the lake by Joseph Wright of Derby, are particularly powerful. There's also a re-creation of a yeoman-farmer's kitchen-living room, bits and bobs of Wordsworth memorabilia, and displays on the major characters who came within his orbit such as Coleridge and Charles Lamb.

Dove Cottage and the Wordsworth Museum are just off the A591 at Town End, Grasmere. Tel: 05394 35544/35547
Opening times: daily 9am-5.30pm except mid-Jan to mid-Feb
Admission: adult £3.50; child £1.60
The Children's Quizbook, asking questions on the house and museum, is good value at 50p

 The Wordsworth Trust also runs the **Dove Cottage Tea Shop and Restaurant** next to the car park, an excellent place to have lunch or just sink into one of the comfy armchairs with a newspaper (or even a copy of *The Prelude*). The main galleried room is scattered with low chairs and tables, and the coffee is very good cappuccino and espresso, as well as hot chocolate with whipped cream. Through an arch is the main eating area which manages to combine formal place settings with an anything-goes atmosphere. The open sandwiches (smoked salmon, sliced herrings in Madeira sauce, peanut, celery and sweetcorn) are served on thick home-made wholemeal bread, or there's an imaginative hot menu chalked on the blackboard. The sticky toffee pudding is the size of a housebrick and comes with fresh dairy cream. In summer open daily 10.30am-5.30pm (last orders 8.15pm Friday-Sunday); more limited hours in winter.

EASEDALE

Not for nothing did Dorothy Wordsworth call this beautiful valley the Black Quarter for it rains a lot here and the skies always seem to hang heavy. Dorothy's diary records that she and William would walk here almost every day, more often than not having to turn back because of the weather - and on one occasion 'were turned back in the open field by the sight of a cow'. To reach Easedale take the road north-west from Broadgate in Grasmere village by a pretty whitewashed cottage. There's a car park half a mile up the road next to a small, incongruously modern housing estate. Continue on the road as far as a stone bridge at a confluence of streams. The stony path beyond crosses a flat field. At the head of the valley is the waterfall of Sour Milk Gill, known to the Wordsworths as Churn Milk Force, and according to Dorothy 'like a broad stream of snow' in the distance. Beyond the gate at the end of the field the path climbs past the waterfall and reaches a bank overlooking Easedale Tarn. You'll need decent walking shoes and clothing, but the walk is memorable - in Dorothy's words, 'The quietness and still seclusion of the valley affected me even to producing the deepest melancholy.'

Easedale, as popular with walkers now as it was with William and Dorothy Wordsworth

☆ GRASMERE VILLAGE

Many people - too many - regard Grasmere as quintessential lakeland and come here out of a sense of vague obligation. And like other towns and villages in the Lake District, it is a frustratingly unstructured place to walk round, with no square or obvious focal point to mark its centre. The result is that visitors tend to circle aimlessly. Again, the National Park's illustrated leaflet, available from the **Tourist Information Centre** in Red Bank Road (tel: 05394 35245) is the best bet for finding your way around. The TIC is open daily Easter to end October.

The **Parish Church of St Oswald** and its graveyard by the River Rothay are a must, and not just because of the graves of the Wordsworths, simple and moving as these are. They rest in the shade of one of the eight yew trees planted by Wordsworth himself. His and wife Mary's headstone bears the simple inscription: 'William Wordsworth, 1850. Mary Wordsworth, 1859'. Nearby are the graves of Dorothy, of their children, and of Hartley Coleridge. Another feature of the graveyard is its three separate entrances that once served three different parishes - the lych gate to the north for Grasmere, the west gate for Langdale, and the arched gate to the south for Rydal and Ambleside.

The oldest parts of the church date from the 13th century though it is nondescript from the outside (the roughcast finish is 19th century). The interior is fascinating, however. The nave is bisected by a series of two-tiered white-washed arches - this was the original outer wall before the north aisle was added in the last decade of the 15th century - and the roof consists of what Wordsworth called 'naked rafters intricately crossed'.

The aroma emanating from the tiny building next to the lych gate is the smell of freshly baked ginger bread and rum butter and fudge, for this is the famous **Sara Nelson's Gingerbread Shop**. This tiny cottage served as the village school (from 1685 to 1854) before Ms Nelson made a killing selling gingerbread to Victorians visiting Wordsworth's grave. Inside there's a single counter piled high with goodies. The gingerbread, still made according to Sara Nelson's recipe, is sold by the slice, and delicious it is too. The shop is open Monday-Saturday 9.30am-5.30pm, Sunday 12.30-5.30pm all year round, though it tends to close at dusk in the winter.

Stock Lane, the road to the A591at the south end of the village, is lined with the usual shops selling knitwear, walking gear, furry animals and the like. **Craglands of Grasmere**, which sells knitwear, fabrics and jewellery, would be unremarkable but for the fact that it also stocks lovely sweaters made by the John Smedley company, purveyors of pukka pullies for 200 years. The shop is open daily all year round.

At the north end of the village on Broadgate is the **Heaton Cooper Studio**, a permanent exhibition of watercolours and prints by the Lake District's most popular artists, W Heaton Cooper and his father A Heaton Cooper. There's scarcely a lake, fell or tarn that hasn't been commited to paper by these prolific painters, and certainly if you like this kind of naturalistic painting you could hardly do better. But there's something rather mechanical and invariable about the execution, and the few works here by Julian Cooper, son of W Heaton Cooper, are more interesting. Still, if you're looking for some decent watercolours for the wall this is the place to come. The smallest prints cost about £2 unframed, £13 framed; the largest prints are about £18 unframed, £95 framed. Originals cost £500-£1000. There's a framing shop on the premises so you can choose what you want. There's also a wide selection of greetings cards. The Studio is open daily all year.

Further north up Broadgate on the right hand side is **Barney's Newsbox**, an innocent-looking newsagent that happens to have the biggest jigsaw selection in England, if not the universe. 'A lot of the walking types seem to like jigsaws,' says owner David Perrem. 'There seems to be some connection.' The puzzles, all 4,000 of them, are stored floor to ceiling in the room upstairs and the selection ranges from *Gone with the Wind* to Ingres' *Odalisque* by way of the Chippendales and includes the World's Most Difficult Jigsaw Puzzle, a double-sided monster with the same image on both sides rotated through 90 degrees. A mail order catalogue is also available. Being a newsagent, Barney's Newsbox is open every day 7am-6pm.

To get away from the crowds, there's a pleasant walk along the banks of the River Rothay with seats along the way for taking the weight off your feet. Pick up the path next to Sara Nelson's Gingerbread Shop, pass behind the churchyard and loop back round along the inner bank of the river. Cross a bridge to the opposite bank, follow the river round to the right and cross another bridge to the Broadgate Meadow car park. Here there's a runic cross that serves as a war memorial, a children's playground and lots of space for a picnic.

⊗ LANGDALES DRIVE

 The Langdales, Great and Little, are the true heart of the Lake District, encompassing its most distinctive skyline - the twin Elephant Man peaks of the Langdale Pikes - ending in a vast bowl that climbs to the majestic heights of Crinkle Crags, Bow Fell and the Scafells. From Ambleside take the A593 to Coniston and turn off at Skelwith Bridge. Alternatively, there is a back route from Grasmere which is much more scenic. It starts on Red Bank Road beyond the Tourist Information Centre and car park. Follow the road up behind Grasmere Lake, ignoring the turning to the left, and drop down towards either Elterwater or Chapel Stile (either road will do). On the descent good views are to be had of the head of the valley with the Pikes, called Harrison Stickle and Pike of Stickle, predominant as always. Both roads lead to the B5343. Turn right onto it and keep going. The village of Chapel Stile is not a place to spend time in. The terrace of modern houses as you leave the village looks impossibly out of place, especially when sheep are grazing on the lawns.

Just beyond the New Dungeon Ghyll Hotel is the Stickle Barn car park, from which you can climb to **Stickle Tarn** alongside Stickle Gyhll. The ascent is steep, especially in the latter stages when it involves a bit of scrambling over rocks. But it is worth it for the sudden view of the tarn, whose placidity mocks one's exertions to get there, and the brooding forehead of rock called Pavey Ark which overlooks it. Dorothy Wordsworth records in her Grasmere journals that on September 2, 1800 her brother climbed this path in the company of his brother John and Coleridge.

Past the Old Dungeon Ghyll Hotel (see Where to Stay) the road turns abruptly left and climbs steeply across some cattle grids. On the way up there are excellent views back of the flat green valley bottom and the khaki fells stitched neatly to it by hedgerows. The road continues past **Blea Tarn**, one of the finest low level tarns in the Lakes. There's a car park on the east side of the road and the walk to the tarn takes about ten minutes. Blea Tarn is an unusual combination of the wild and woolly and the prettified, with a landscaped woodland on its west side to offset the bleak moorland around it. Someone at some stage has taken the trouble to plant azaleas here, and set out paths among the firs and Scots pines. A rocky headland veined like the back of a hand with tree roots makes a good place to pause and drink in the beauty of it all. The view across to the Langdale Pikes from the foot of the tarn is another visual cliché of lakeland, and understandably so.

The road continues to a sharp junction with the road to Wrynose Pass. Turn left here for **Little Langdale** past Little Langdale Tarn. The road along the valley is a frustrating one, extremely narrow and with few passing places and none to stop and enjoy the gentle lushness of Great Langdale's little sister. Continue past the Three Shires Inn and at the bottom of a steep descent, turn left and follow the road into the village of **Elterwater**. If you know what's good for you, pause at the pub by the village green.

The **Britannia Inn** is long, low and white-washed, with pretty window boxes, tables and chairs on the terrace, and a snug bar. The food is above average pub fare - Cumberland pie (spicy shepherd's pie), Cumberland sausage, local trout, all with peas and chips or baked potatoes, good salads, and generous ploughman's and quarryman's (with chicken liver pâté) lunches. Food is served 12-2pm and 6.30-9pm (Sundays 7-9pm) all year round.

The Britannia Inn by the village green in Elterwater

South of the pub by the bridge you can pick up the riverside path that takes you to the small lake, **Elter Water**, that gives its name to the village. If you're feeling reasonably lively you can continue on a circular walk of four miles or so that takes in the two waterfalls that siphon off the water from the Langdale valleys. After passing the north-eastern corner of Elter Water (a rather boring body of water, if truth be told), the path continues along the bank of the River Brathay to **Skelwith Force**, a short but powerful waterfall. The path goes through a slate quarry yard to the main road, the A593. Turn right across the bridge, follow the road round to the right, then go right again in front of some cottages. The path goes through a wood and farmyard, then passes to the left of a farmhouse before crossing a field and dropping steeply to a stile on a minor road. Cross the stile a little way up on the other side of the road to reach **Colwith Force**, some 40 feet high. Return to the minor road, turn left and keep going for about a mile to get back to Elterwater village.

RYDAL AND GRASMERE WALK

This may usefully be known as the Wordsworth Walk, for it takes in Dove Cottage and Rydal Mount, the poet's two most famous homes, as well as the beautiful Rydal Water and Grasmere, the two lakes most closely associated with him. The circuit is about five miles, and can be stretched to take up the best part of a day if you choose to include visits to Dove Cottage and Rydal rather than doing them separately.

Use the car park just south of Rydal off the A591, a right turn over a small bridge and right again over a cattlegrid. From the car park follow the road up and take the gate in a wall opposite some cottages. Cross a meadow to Rydal Woods, then follow the shore of Rydal Water. On the opposite shore fronting the A591 is Nab Cottage, former home of De Quincey and Hartley Coleridge. The path takes you away from the lake up by a stone wall then steepens to a ridge. Continue on the rising path to the left to Loughrigg Terrace with excellent views of Grasmere and Helm Crag behind the village. Then retrace your steps and drop down to the southerly end of Grasmere, where swans backpeddle at the edge of a shallow weir. There's a beach on the shore that gets very busy in summer, and views across to the Prince of Wales Hotel on the eastern shore. The island in the middle of Grasmere is like a Victorian etching, with Scots pines and a mossy ruin, though in Wordsworth's day, when he, Dorothy

➜

and Coleridge went there for picnics, it was bald and used for sheep grazing.

Half-way round Grasmere, the path turns sharp left away from the lake and joins Red Bank Road (one of the routes over into Langdale) to reach Grasmere village. Turn right in front of the church and follow Stock Lane to the A591. On the other side of the main road take the left fork, the old turnpike road, past Dove Cottage. Notice the grates low down in the walls of some of the houses on the right-hand side - this was where the traditional ashpit toilets, what Dorothy Wordsworth called 'The Necessity', were emptied. At the top by a pond is the farmstead of How Top, a typical lakeland farm with a good example of a 'bank' barn.

Grasmere

Turn left by the pond on the course of the Old Corpse Road, used to take bodies from Rydal to Grasmere for burial before Rydal had a church. The road narrows to a footpath by a house called Brockstone. The escarpment above is strewn with boulders and bleached dead trees before the path opens out along a meadow with the A591 and Rydal Water below. When you reach the road at the end turn right past Rydal Mount and descend to the A591. Turn left and take the first right back to the car park.

Boats are available for hire on Grasmere from Mrs Allonby, The Boat Landing, Red Bank Road (tel: 05394 35409): £2.50 an hour for 1 person, £6 for 4. Boating is not permitted on Rydal Water. Both lakes are fished for pike, perch and eels: permits from Tourist Information Centres

Rydal Mount, where Wordsworth lived for 37 years until his death

☆ RYDAL MOUNT

This is where Wordsworth spent the last 37 years of his life. By the time he died here in 1850 he had achieved the status of a national monument. The poet who had thrilled to the French Revolution and broken the mould of poetic sensibility settled into a cosy domesticity in his later years, pottering in his garden like any senior citizen and showing more concern for petunias than pentameters. For this reason Rydal Mount feels more like one of those comfortable and discreet country house hotels that are tucked away all over the Lakes than a workshop of high art. The accessible rooms - dining room, library, study and bedrooms - are rather disappointing, especially after Dove Cottage, even if the 'table tennis bat' information boards are available in a babel of languages, from Afrikaans to Singhalese and Esperanto.

But it was the four-acre garden that was Wordsworth's pride and joy, and it remains a lovely place to walk in. It includes a summerhouse, where Wordsworth composed poetry, the far terrace where he recited it aloud, and the 9th-century Mound, crowned with scrubs screening a seat, which was used to light beacon fires to warn of attack by marauding Scots. There are some rare trees and shrubs, notably a fern leaf beech introduced by the poet which is apparently ungrowable except by grafting it onto a newly planted beech tree - which begs the question of where the first one came from. And there are badgers, which come nightfall turn into rotary cultivators, churning deep furrows in the otherwise immaculate lawns. They would have tested Wordsworth's love of nature to breaking point.

Rydal Mount is just off the A591 between Ambleside and Grasmere. Tel: 05394 33002
Opening times: Nov-Feb daily except Tues 10am-4pm; Mar-Oct daily 9.30am-5pm
Admission: adult £2; child 80p

WHERE TO STAY

Easedale
🏠 🕺 🐴 ▭ £££

Lancrigg, Easedale, *Grasmere,*
Cumbria LA22 9QN
Tel: 05394 35317
Open all year

According to the Jason Donovan look-alike (and sound-alike) at the reception desk, 'Wordsworth got his inspiration from looking out of these windows' up the valley of Easedale. Certainly this lovely country house hotel with its traditional cylindrical Lakeland chimneys has some distinguished associations. It was once the home of Arctic explorer John Richardson, now buried in Grasmere churchyard, and Wordsworth and Dorothy came here when they lived at nearby Allan Bank. Now it has a distinguished reputation not just for its incomparable setting, in 27 acres of Easedale, but for its fine, exclusively vegetarian cooking.

The rooms are priced according to size and amenities - the cheapest have shared bathrooms, and the dearest have four-poster beds and whirlpool baths - but no two are alike and all are done out with flair and style. The pick of the bunch is the 30-foot-long Booth-Richardson Room (the explorer's former library), with its own door into the garden, plasterwork ceiling and free-standing bath

(curtained off) in the room itself. A typical evening meal might start with Greek marinated vegetables and feta cheese, followed by spinach sesame soup, stuffed vine leaves, and apricot and tofu 'cheesecake', while the imaginative breakfasts include a choice of vegetarian kedgeree or buckwheat pancakes with maple syrup. Smoking in bedrooms only.

Grasmere
🏠 🕺 ▭ ££

How Foot Hotel, *Town End,*
Grasmere, Cumbria LA22 9SQ
Tel: 05394 35366
Open all year

Adjacent to Dove Cottage, How Foot is owned by the Wordsworth Trust and is the former home of the Cookson family, close friends of the Wordsworths, as well of the Rev Spooner of 'spoonerism' fame. There are plans, still a few years away from realisation, to turn it into a library to house the Trust's expanding collection of books. This is presumably why it remains in a state of genteel dilapidation that gives it an atmosphere somewhere between a youth hostel and a seaside guesthouse that has seen better days. This is rather refreshing after the preponderance of Laura Ashley in so many Lakeland hotels, for if it is nothing else How

Foot is relaxing and comfortable, and the staff youthful and extremely informal without being inefficient. There are six en suite rooms, all with colour TV and radio alarm clock and, although there are no evening meals, the breakfasts are a speciality: locally baked bread, hand-cured bacon, Mr Woodall's finest sausages from Waberthwaite. Another interesting feature is the paintings, borrowed from the Wordsworth Museum and hung in rotation. Smoking in the lounge only.

Langdale

🏕 🏊 🐕

Green Howe Caravan Park,
Great Langdale, Ambleside,
Cumbria LA22 9JU
Tel: 09667 231
Open Mar 1 - mid-Nov
A superb location in the heart of Great Langdale, in the shadow of those stunning Pikes, and though the caravans win no aesthetic prizes (they look like green biscuit tins) the setting, amenities and personal service offered by owners John Holden and son Graham more than compensate. The site is cut into the fellside and built on terraces, the most spectacular hanging vertiginously over the road. There's a shop (with off-licence), newspaper delivery service, laundry, and children's playground, and the caravans (ranging from four to eight berths) are all equipped with gas fires, gas cookers, fridges, hot and cold water, showers and colour TV. Unsurprisingly, Green Howe is an habitual winner of the English Tourist Board's Rose Award for consistently high standards.

Langdale

🏠 ✕ 🏊 🐎 ▭ ££

The Old Dungeon Ghyll Hotel,
Great Langdale, Ambleside,
Cumbria LA22 9JY
Tel: 09667 272
Open all year
The hotel brochure shows a panoramic view of the head of Great Langdale, with the whitewashed Old Dungeon Ghyll nestling in one corner of the green valley bottom below Harrison Stickle, as it has for 300 years. Along with the Wasdale Head Inn, this is the most famous mountaineers' and walkers' hotel in the country. They have centuries of experience of catering for fellwalkers and it shows in the surroundings and services - extremely comfortable, friendly and efficient without a hint of stuffiness. Not that you have to be a walker to stay here - there are plenty of other attractions - but it would be a shame not to experience the magnificent local landscape while you're here. There are 14 bedrooms, just four of them en suite, but the shared bathrooms have masses of hot water for soaking tired limbs, and the iron bedsteads are a delight. If you're looking for undiluted peace and tranquillity avoid the four rooms above the walkers' bar which is rather noisy in the evenings. (See also Where to Eat.)

Rydal

🏠 🏊 🐎 🚫 £

Nab Cottage, *Rydal, Ambleside,*
Cumbria LA22 9SD
Tel: 05394 35311
Open all year
Another guesthouse/hotel with intriguing literary associations, the ancient and picturesque Nab Cottage is the former home of both Hartley

Coleridge, the poet's wayward son, and Thomas De Quincey, essayist and opium eater. Unfortunately the busy A591 interposes itself between the cottage and the beautiful Rydal Water but, quite apart from its resonant links with the past, Nab Cottage retains sufficient of its original quaintness to provide a memorable retreat. There are seven rooms, all understandably small given the age of the place (it was built in 1702), all centrally heated and just two with private bathrooms. There's a TV lounge and a larger lounge with open fire and books of local history, including a folder of the history of the cottage itself. Breakfast and evening meals (served at 7pm and not included in the basic price) are prepared on an Aga cooker in the old kitchen.

WHERE TO EAT

Ambleside

Bertram's Restaurant, *Market Place, Ambleside*
Tel: 05394 32119
Open daily from 6pm; closed last 3 wks Jan

Centrally located in what used to be Ambleside's meat market, Bertram's is a relaxed bistro-type place with functional tables and black and white tiled floor in an interesting architectural setting - white-painted iron pillars, beamed ceiling, thick walls and triangular-topped windows. Mel and John Tennant from Leeds have been in charge here since 1987 - John wears the pinny and Mel turns on the charm front of house. There's an emphasis on pizzas, but plenty of other dishes too - swordfish, steaks, pasta, vegetarian bake - and children can share a main dish or just stick with a starter: soup, pâté, smoked salmon. There's a comprehensive range of trendy foreign lagers: Becks, San Miguel, Labatts, Tiger, Grolsch and Sapporo. The food is decent enough but what really makes Bertram's is the atmosphere - subdued lighting and nightlights on the tables - and the friendly service.

Children are allowed until 7pm only. Last orders: 10pm (10.30pm May-October).

Ambleside
✗ 🍽 ££

Zeffirelli's, *Compston Road, Ambleside*
Tel: 05394 33845
Open all year for dinner from 5pm plus lunch Sat & Sun

This is an unusual and worthy venture for a small town like Ambleside (pop 5,000), a complex of cinema/theatre, bar, shops, café and restaurant. This is apparently Ken Russell's favourite small cinema and there's no doubting the excellence of the restaurant, which bills itself as a 'wholefood pizzeria'. The decor is startling, a risky combination of minimalist Japanese red and black, art deco and cinematic chic (portraits of film stars, broken-down projectors) that somehow works to create a delightful ambience. The pizzas, all with wholemeal base and vegetarian toppings, are delicious as well as being as big and upholstered as cushions. A good place to make an evening of it by taking in a film before or after eating. Last orders: dinner 9.45pm; lunch at weekends 2pm.

Langdale
🏠 ✕ 🛏 £££

The Old Dungeon Ghyll Hotel,
Great Langdale, Ambleside
Tel: 09667 272
Open all year: R dinner only (one sitting); bar lunch and dinner from 6pm
There's an option here - the one-sitting, limited-choice restaurant menu served in the parquet-floored dining room with linen tablecoths, or bar food served in the rough and ready walkers' bar in the old cowshed (the stalls are still there), where the lino is as rugged as the fells, the whitewashed walls are decorated with old climbing photographs and a bizarre mural of a man with the DTs, and the magnificent old range keeps you snug and toasty. Either way the food is a delight. A typical restaurant menu might start with celery soup followed by a choice of melon or potted char, then poussin or game casserole, and fruit pie or hazelnut and strawberry roulade. In the bar, the emphasis is on volume - pizzas, vegetable curry, jumbo sausages, washed down with a choice of real beer, Theakston's, Marston's Pedigree or Pendle Witches' Brew (go easy on the latter). Restaurant: one sitting for dinner at 7.30pm. Bar - last orders: lunch 2pm; dinner 8.30pm.

Skelwith Bridge
🏠 ✕ 🛏 ££

Skelwith Bridge Hotel, *nr Ambleside*
Tel: 05394 34254
Bridge Restaurant open all year dinner only; Talbot Inn lunch from 11.30am (late Sept-Easter 12pm) and dinner from 6.30pm (Sun 7pm)
The Skelwith Bridge is at an historic junction, where the road to Great Langdale branches from the A593 to Coniston. The Bridge Restaurant prides itself - with good reason - on its English and French cooking. The fixed-price menu changes daily and might include prawn and mushroom skillet or savoury vol-au-vents for starters, followed by consommé Julienne or orange sorbet, with a main course choice of plaice caprice (baked with bananas and breadcrumbs), pork Diane, roast guinea fowl or vegetable biryani. There's always a 'wine of the week' and the wine list has some 60 choices from around the world. If you fancy eating more informally, the Talbot Inn, which is part of the hotel and opened in 1991 as a re-creation of a pub on the same site, has good bar food chalked up on a blackboard: Cumberland hotpot and baked potato, steak and ale pie, and, for the truly famished, 12-inch Cumberland sausage. Last orders: Bridge Restaurant - dinner 9pm; Talbot Inn - lunch 2.30pm (late Sept-Easter 2pm); dinner 9pm.